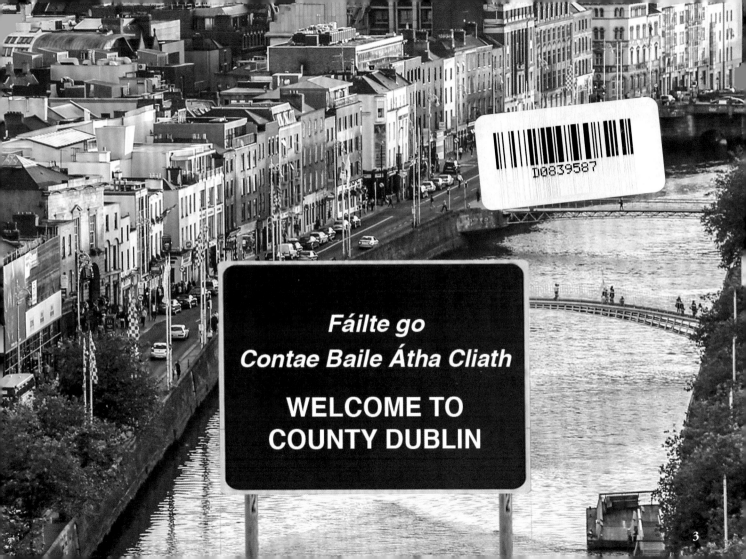

Fáilte go
Contae Baile Átha Cliath

WELCOME TO
COUNTY DUBLIN

D0839587

Contents

Key to abbreviations:
(PD) = Public Domain (FI) = Fáilte Ireland (OPW) = Office of Public Works
(A.I.F) = Another Interesting Fact (I) = Insert
(GPO) = The General Post Office

There is an ancient Irish legend that tells the story of Abhartach, an evil chieftain, who was betrayed by his subjects. To seek revenge, every night he would rise from his grave to drink the blood of his subjects. The famous *Dracula* author, Bram Stoker, brought these stories and others to a whole new dimension, instilling fear into the lives of generations. Abraham 'Bram' Stoker (1847-1912) was born at Marino Crescent, Clontarf, in Dublin. As a young child, Stoker suffered ill-health and his mother is believed to have told him horror stories while he recovered. Having studied at Trinity College, Dublin, he began working as a civil servant at Dublin Castle. Bram married Florence Balcombe, his neighbour (and former girlfriend of Oscar Wilde (see #42). Stoker's real-life inspiration for his character *Dracula* was modelled on his lifelong friend, the famous actor Henry Irving. Stoker and his new wife moved to London where he accepted a job as Irving's personal secretary and business manager of the Lyceum Theatre. They had one son, Irving Noel.

After several years research on European folklore and mythological stories of vampires, Stoker wrote *Dracula* in 1897. The novel is set in Eastern Europe with Dracula's castle located in Transylvania. Dracul in the Romanian language can mean 'dragon or devil'. Sheridan Le Fanu's novel *Carmilla* (see #61) and the crypts in St. Michan's Church (see #87) also influenced Stoker in his storyline. Bram Stoker died in 1912, he was cremated and his ashes are on display at Golders Green Crematorium, London.

Left: Abraham 'Bram' Stoker (PD)
Right: Stoker's creation "Dracula" (Shutterstock)
Insert: First edition cover of the book (PD)

The Phoenix Park is five times the size of Hyde Park in London and twice as big as Central Park in New York. The name of the park has no association with the mythical bird, the Phoenix, but is derived from the Irish name 'Páirc an Fhionn-Uisce' meaning 'the park of the clear water.' It is one of the largest urban enclosed parks in Europe, with a circumference of 12k (7mls) and total area 707 hectares (1,752 acres). It was established in 1662 as a royal deer park and was stocked with a herd of wild fallow deer, their descendants still roam freely to this day. Other features in Phoenix Park include ornamental gardens, nature trails and broad expanses of grassland separated by avenues of trees. The main attractions within the park include; the residence of the Irish president - Áras an Uachtaráin, the official Irish State guest house - Farmleigh House and the Dublin Zoological Gardens (see #18).

Several Viking graves and bronze brooches were discovered near the Islandbridge edge of the park and it is believed to be the biggest Viking cemetery outside of Scandinavia.

Left: Deer in the Phoenix Park (Shay Connolly)
Right: Expansive view of the Phoenix Park (Thomas Mulchi)

#03   *A Nobel Prize and an Oscar*

George Bernard Shaw (1856-1950), dramatist, socialist and critic was born in Upper Synge Street, Dublin. He is the only person in the world to have a Nobel Prize and an Oscar. He wrote more than 60 plays, 5 novels, dozens of stories and essays and over 250,000 letters. He was awarded the Nobel Prize for Literature in 1925. He wrote the play *Pygmalion* in 1912 which became better known world-wide as the musical *My Fair Lady*, and he bequeathed the royalties to the National Gallery of Ireland. In 1938 he received an Oscar for *Pygmalion*. Other notable works written by G.B. Shaw were *Fanny's First Play* (1911) and his internationally successful play *St. Joan* (1923). In 1946 he became an Honorary Freeman of Dublin City. Because of his strong beliefs he refused many other awards, including the offer of a knighthood. Most of his writings featured social problems with a hint of comedy. Shaw wrote extensively on the issues of education, religion, government, marriage, healthcare and class privilege.

Left: George Bernard Shaw Relaxing at home (PD)
Right: G.B. Shaw taking notes (PD)

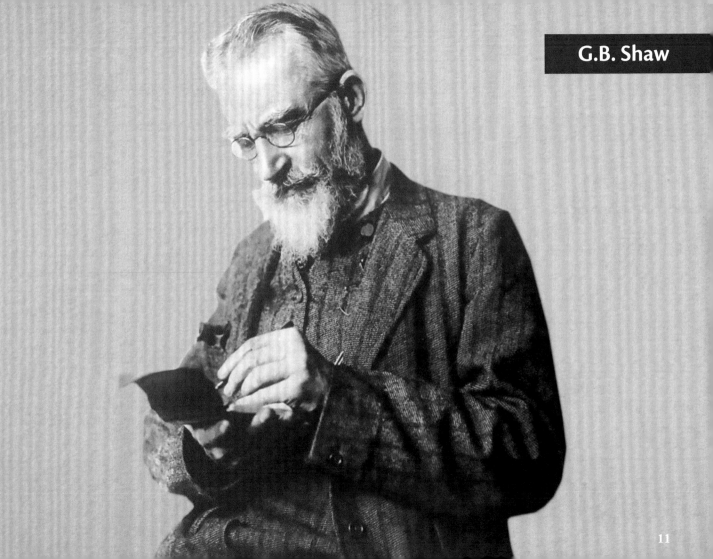

G.B. Shaw

#04   *The Irish Red Setter Dog*

The breed standard for the Irish Red Setter was set up in Dublin in 1886. It was the first time the 'Setter' had become a distinct breed in its own right. The Irish Setter was bred for hunting, especially game birds, which it would locate and 'set or point' in the direction of the prey. The setter has an excellent sense of smell, great stamina and is a tireless and wide-ranging hunter. It is well-suited to fields as well as wet or dry moorland terrain. The setter is also a highly efficient retriever of the game bird. The first setters were a mix of colours; very red or red and white or even lemon coloured. However with its popularity at dog shows the trending preference was for a solid red chestnut colour. The Irish Setter was brought to the USA in the early 19th century and its numbers have increased dramatically. It continues to be a top attraction at all the major dog shows.

Left and Right: The Irish Red Setter in all its glory. (Mark Thomas)

Red Setter

When the 1916 Easter Rising took place one of the first things the British did was cut the telephone and telegraph lines to prevent the Volunteers from communicating with anyone who might support them. Up to this point, wireless signals were always sent from one station to a specific receiving station. No one had yet tried sending a signal into the atmosphere for anyone with a receiver to pick up the message. The Volunteers did just that. They seized the Wireless School of Telegraphy near the GPO, erected aerials, repaired the old equipment and began broadcasting in Morse Code to anyone who might receive the signal. The message was *"Irish Republic declared in Dublin today, Irish troops have captured the city and are in full possession. Enemy cannot move in the city. The whole country rising."* The signal was received in Germany and Bulgaria, passing ships picked up the broadcast and it was relayed to America. The American papers ran with the story 'Revolt in Ireland', but by the end of the week the revolt was over. This transmission is generally accepted as the world's first radio broadcast not aimed at a specific target.

Left: Radio operator (National Library of Ireland)
Right: Radio equipment in use at the time (PD)

Cedric Gibbons (1893-1960) was born in Dublin, moved to the United States at the turn of the century and later studied art at the Art Students League of New York. He began working in films for Edison Studios in 1915 and three years later went to MGM as the Art Director, where he remained for 32 years. He was one of the original founding members of The Academy of Motion Pictures and it has been argued that Gibbons was one of the most important art directors in the history of American Cinema. He designed the Academy Awards statuette and proudly collected 11 of them himself. He was Art Director for over 150 movies. He died in Hollywood at the age of 67 and is buried in Los Angeles.

Other Dublin recipients of Oscars include: Glen Hansard for the song *Falling Slowly* from the movie *Once*; Brenda Fricker for her role as Christy Brown's mother in *My Left Foot* (see #56); Barry Fitzgerald for his role in *Going My Way*; George Bernard Shaw for *Pygmalion* (see #56). Maureen O'Hara won an Honorary Achievement Award; Richie Baneham for visual effects in *Avatar* and Ben Cleary for best live action short *Stutterer*.

Left: Glen Hansard and Marketa Irglova accept their Oscars for the Dublin based movie **'Once'**
Right: Preparing the set for the Academy Awards (Dreamstime)

Oscar Statuette

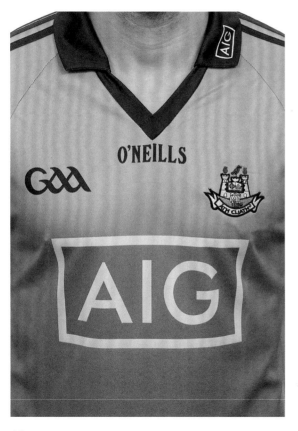

Between 2003 and 2004 the Dublin County Board of the Gaelic Athletic Association began the process to copyright the Dublin crest that was in use, but the crest was declared to be in the public domain. The County Board set about designing a new crest which they could copyright and register as a trade mark. They drew on the county's historical past to create the new crest for all their Football and Hurling teams.

1. Three castles in flames – signifying the city of Dublin
2. A Raven – representing the area of Fingal
3. Viking Longboat – signifying the county area of Dun Laoghaire-Rathdown
4. A Book – representing the South Dublin area.
5. The name Áth Cliath (in Irish) replaces the 'Dublin' name on previous crests

The sky blue colour was adopted in 1918, but the collar and shorts were white and the socks were hooped in white and blue. The present look of sky blue jersey with dark blue shorts appeared in 1974. The Dublin team are often called 'The Dubs,' 'The Jacks' and 'The Boys in Blue.'

Left: Crest as it looks on a county jersey
Right: Details of the crest (Dublin County GAA Board)

1

2

3

4

5

ÁTH CLIATH ®

The movie *Michael Collins* is an historical biopic of the controversial life and death of Michael Collins who led the Irish Republican Army (IRA) in their struggle against the British Empire. It was written and directed by Neil Jordan. It was filmed in 1996 and starred Liam Neeson, Alan Rickman, Aidan Quinn, Stephen Rea, Brendan Gleeson and Julia Roberts. Film locations included; The Four Courts, Kilmainham Gaol, The GPO and Dublin Castle.

Far and Away (1992) starring Tom Cruise and Nicole Kidman had some scenes shot in Temple Bar, where the cobble stone streets doubled as Boston, Massachusetts. The beautiful grounds of Trinity College was the setting for the 1983 comedy-drama *Educating Rita*, which starred Michael Caine and Julie Walters.

The life of Dublin criminal Martin Cahill featured in 2 movies: *The General* (1998), directed by John Boorman, starred Brendan Gleeson and Jon Voight. It was shot in several city locations. The second movie was released in 2000, *Ordinary Decent Criminal* and starred Kevin Spacey and Colin Farrell. The director was Thaddeus O'Sullivan. Oscar winning *Once* (2007) starring Glen Hansard and Markéta Irglová, directed by John Carney was shot mostly in city centre locations including Grafton Street and Georges Street. The Alan Parker movie *The Commitments* (1991) saw Colm Meaney star alongside a young Glen Hansard.

Left: Liam Neeson was excellent in his role of Michael Collins (Shutterstock)
Right: Julia Roberts played Kitty Kiernan in *Michael Collins* (Dreamstime)
Centre: Michael Caine starred in *Educating Rita* (Dreamstime)
Far Right: Tom Cruise and Nicole Kidman in *Far and Away* (Shutterstock)

21

John G. Rathborne Ltd. is the oldest firm in Dublin, dating back to 1488. The Rathbornes are manufacturers of a range of candles, varying from paraffin-wax to pure beeswax. In the 13th century candle making was confined to the rich, many of whom used beeswax from their own hives. The poor used rush-lights which were not very long lasting. The Rathborne's developed a method of candle-making which made the candles available to the poor as well as the rich. 'You could not hold a candle to it' is an old Irish expression that is still used today, meaning something is beautiful or at its best and this saying shows the high esteem in which candles were held. In the 17th century the Rathborne's were contracted to supply street lighting in Dublin, this was followed by the contract to supply candles to the lighthouses around the Irish coast.

In 1966 the Rathborne's acquired Lalor Candles Limited, a company that was noted for church candles. Church candles are made of beeswax and they are still made in the same traditional way as centuries ago.

The candle making firm started their business near St. Werburgh's Church before moving to Stoneybatter, Parnell Street, East Wall and now Blanchardstown.

Left: Making the church candle
Right: (top): Manufacturing through the years
(bottom) A sample of the candle range. (Rathbornes and Lalors candles)

RATHBORNES

FOUNDED IN DUBLIN

ESTABLISHED

1488

Alcock and Brown completed the first non-stop west to east flight across the Atlantic in 1919, flying from Newfoundland, Canada to Clifden, County Galway. It was not until April 1928 that the first east to west transatlantic flight was successfully completed. Co-pilot on this flight was Dublin born Colonel James Fitzmaurice. Also on board the aircraft 'The Bremen' on the historical flight were two Germans - Captain Hermann Koehl and Baron von Huenefeld. The east to west flight was a more difficult challenge due to the prevailing winds over the Atlantic. It took off from Baldonnell, County Dublin on 12th April and after 36.5 hours flying landed on a frozen pond on Greenly Island between Labrador and Newfoundland.

The achievement of the Irish and German airmen was greeted so enthusiastically by the Americans that nearly 2 million people lined the victory parade in their honour down Broadway and 5th Avenue. Former U.S President Calvin Coolidge presented the three airmen with the U.S. Distinguished Flying Cross for "heroism or extraordinary achievement while participating in an aerial flight." They were the first foreigners ever to have received the award. They were also given the freedom of New York City and Dublin City. There is a granite strip on New York City's Broadway commemorating Fitzmaurice and the crew. 'The Bremen' aircraft is now completely restored and belongs to the Henry Ford Museum in Dearborn, Michigan. It is currently on display at the Bremen Airport Museum in Germany.

Left: James Fitzmaurice shakes hands with Major Nichols in Boston
Right: (top left) The pilots are introduced to the Boston crowd (top right) The Bremen on Greenly Island (bottom left) The pilots in the New York parade (bottom right) The crew pose for the New York crowd (All photos courtesy of Bob Cullum, Monica Shin, The Boston Public Library and the Leslie Jones Collection)

The origin of the expression 'Chancing your arm' (taking a risk) goes back to 1492. Two Irish families, the Fitzgeralds of Kildare and the Butlers of Ormond, were involved in a raging dispute. The disagreement centred on the appointment of Lord Deputy, a position both families desired. In one of the many skirmishes between the families, the Butlers took refuge in the Chapter House of St. Patricks Cathedral. Fitzgerald, the Earl of Kildare, decided that the dispute needed to end. To show his good faith, he cut a hole in the door of the Chapter House and offered his hand in friendship through the hole. The Butlers, realising the Kildares were serious in their intention, shook hands through the hole in the door and peace was restored. Today the door is known as 'The Door of Reconciliation' and is on display in the Cathedral.

Left: Door of Reconciliation (Dahon)
Right: St Patrick's Cathedral in the summer sunshine (FI)

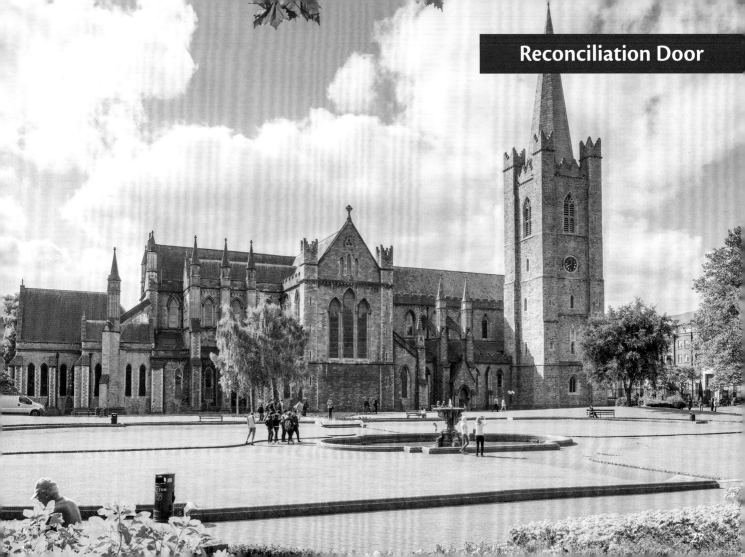

Amhrán na bhFiann

Sinne Fianna Fáil,
atá faoi gheall ag Éirinn,
Buíon dár slua
Thar toinn do ráinig chugainn,
Faoi mhóid bheith saor
Seantír ár sinsear feasta,
Ní fhágfar faoin tíorán ná faoin tráill.
Anocht a théam sa bhearna baoil,
Le gean ar Ghaeil, chun báis nó saoil,
Le gunna scréach faoi lámhach na bpiléar,
Seo libh canaidh amhrán na bhfiann

Peadar Kearney (1883-1942) was born in Lower Dorset Street, Dublin. He was a house painter by trade but he also taught night classes in Irish, Séan O'Casey being one of his pupils. In 1907 he wrote the lyrics for *The Soldiers Song (Amhrán na bhFiann)* while his friend Patrick Heeney wrote the music. During the Easter Rising of 1916 the volunteers used this song as a morale booster for the troops. Kearney was also one of the founder members of the Irish Volunteers and was very active in the fight for Independence. He fought in Jacob's factory under Thomas MacDonagh and was a personal friend of Michael Collins.

In 1926 the Irish Free State adopted *Amhrán na bhFiann* as the Irish National Anthem and in 1933 bought the copyright to the song for £980. The Irish language translation was by Liam Ó Rinn.

Peadar Kearney was buried in Glasnevin Cemetery beside Thomas Ashe and Piaras Béaslaí. Other songs composed by Kearney include: *The Tri-Coloured Ribbon, The Foggy Dew* and *Erin go Brágh*. There is a monument to his memory in Dorset Street.

Left: Words of National Anthem (David Murphy)
Right: The sculpture to honour Peadar Kearney in Lower Dorset Street (William Murphy)
Insert: Peadar Kearney composer of our National Anthem (Glasnevin Trust)

Amrán na bhFiann

1883 – 1942

Peadar Kearney

Here at 68 Lower Dorset Street
Dublin was the birthplace of
Peadar Kearney who wrote the
words for the Irish National
Anthem

#13   *The Borstal Boy*

Brendan Behan, nephew of Peadar Kearney (see #12), was born into a Republican family in Russell Street in 1923. Behan is regarded as one of the greatest Irish writers and his works included poetry, short stories, novels and plays. He left school at the age of 13 and began working with his father as a house painter. He joined the IRA at 16 and set out to bomb Liverpool Docks without clearance from the IRA. He was caught by the British Police and sentenced to 3 years in Borstal, a prison for young offenders. When released, he returned to Dublin and shortly afterwards was sent to Mountjoy prison for the attempted murder of 2 detectives. In prison he studied and became fluent in Irish. In 1954 his play *The Quare Fellow* became a success and the well known Dublin song *The Auld Triangle* comes from this play. In 1958 his best-selling autobiographical novel *Borstal Boy* was published. With this success, Behan was to become more and more dependent on alcohol and was later diagnosed with diabetes. He died in 1964 at the age of 41 and was buried in Glasnevin, the attendance at his funeral was one of the largest ever. He famously said that there was "no bad publicity, only your obituary." There is a bench in his memory along the Royal Canal (see #85) near Drumcondra Road.

Another Interesting Fact (A.I.F): Stephen Behan, Brendan's father was one of Michael Collins' private army known as the 'Twelve Apostles,' who were responsible for assassinating British Army officers during the Anglo-Irish war.

Left: Brendan Behan bench on the banks of the Royal Canal (Michael Foley)
Right: Portrait of Brendan Behan (Pervaneh Matthews)

Pezvan

In 1931 a Dublin pharmacist developed a cream that was primarily aimed as a treatment of nappy rash. It was also used to treat eczema, bedsores, rash and minor skin problems. Thomas Smith, a Professor of Pharmacy and a retail pharmacist, developed the cream at the back of his shop on Old Cabra Road. He called it 'Smith's Baby Cream.' The ingredients consisted of a water-repellent base of oils and waxes, moisturising agent and a weak anaesthetic. The product proved so popular that in the 1940's new manufacturing premises were needed. In the 1950's the name Sudocrem was adopted. Clever marketing of the product in the 1960's increased the popularity of the cream when all new mothers in Ireland were given free samples as they left the maternity hospitals. In the 1980's the brand expanded to Northern Ireland and England and was soon the leading nappy rash cream in both countries. It has been described by consumers as a 'miracle cream' and has many celebrity fans. More products have been added by the company and are available in over 40 countries worldwide. The Sudocrem brand is now owned by Actavis Plc., which is a global multi-billion pharmaceutical company. It is still manufactured in Baldoyle, Dublin.

Left: Thomas Smith who developed the cream
Right: The first pot of Sudocrem and the Sudocrem products that are recognised worldwide. (Actavis Plc and Sudocrem)

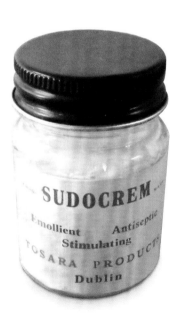

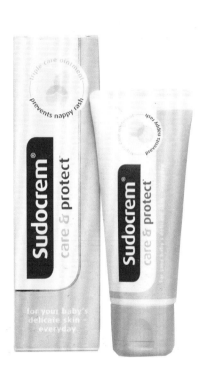

Ireland's Eye is located about 1.5 km (0.9 ml) north of Howth. The Celts called it Eria's Island, this later became Erin's Island until the arrival of the Norsemen, who named it Erin's Ey (Ey was an Old Norse word meaning island). When the Vikings departed, Ireland's Eye was the preferred name. The island is uninhabited and has an area of 24 hectares (60 acres). Its spectacular cliffs on the north-east side provide an excellent sanctuary for seabirds. The Atlantic Puffin is facing the threat of extinction and has been added to the International Union of Conservation of Nature (IUCN). Puffins are regular visitors to Ireland's Eye and their breeding colony is protected.

The Rockabill Island and Maiden Rock, near Dalkey Island, are home to 3 species of tern. They resemble a small sea-gull but have a black cap with a distinctive forked tail and are often called a 'sea swallow.' The Roseate Tern is a critically threatened species and its survival is the main focus of Birdwatch Ireland. The Dalkey Islands are a Special Area of Conservation as the largest European colony of Roseate Tern breed on Rockabill Island. They will only breed where other tern species are nesting, they prefer to nest under cover and have used man-made nest boxes to hatch their young.

Left: Puffins resting on the rocks (Casper Diederik)
Right: The Roseate Tern (Venu Challa)

The Rotunda Hospital in Parnell Square has the unique distinction of being the world's first, and now oldest, maternity hospital. Dr. Bartholomew Mosse (1712-1759) an Irishman, was the founder of the hospital which began its services in Georges Lane (now Fade Street) in 1745 and moved to its present location in 1757. Doctor Mosse qualified as a surgeon and was in charge of soldiers' welfare in Minorca, Spain. After his first wife died in childbirth he focused his attention on midwifery and spent time in Paris developing his knowledge. When he returned to Ireland he was shocked by the mortality rates of infants and mothers during childbirth. He set about raising money, through lotteries and fundraising, for a purpose-built maternity hospital. Mosse invested a large amount of his own money into the project. His fund-raising also benefitted from the charity premiére of Handel's Messiah (see #40). The hospital soon gained an international reputation achieved by the reduction of deaths during childbirth and emphasis on hygiene in the wards. The concert hall used for fund-raising is now the Ambassador Theatre and the hospital's former operating theatre is now the Gate Theatre.

Left: Bartholomew Mosse founder of the Rotunda Hospital (John F. O'Sullivan)
Right: Front of hospital (Michael Bell)
Insert: 250th Anniversary stamp of the Rotunda Hospital (Reproduced by kind permission of An Post)

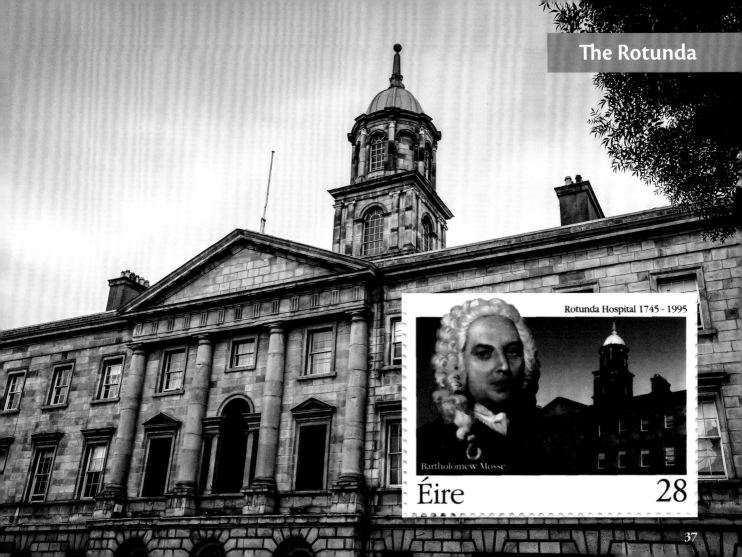

Rotunda Hospital 1745 - 1995

Bartholomew Mosse

Éire

28

In 1750, a French Huguenot brewer called Jean Paul Espinasse fell off his horse while visiting a tavern in Drogheda and died of his injuries. The lease on his brewery in Dublin became available and was taken up 9 years later in 1759 by Arthur Guinness – and thus began the spectacular transformation of the St. James's Gate brewery into the biggest brewery in Europe. The original lease in 1759 to Arthur Guinness was £45 per year for 9,000 years.

It became the largest brewery in Ireland in 1838, and the largest in the world by 1886, with an annual output of 1.2 million barrels. Now no longer the largest brewery in the world, it is still the largest brewer of stout. Over ten million glasses of Guinness - the famous 'black pint' from Dublin - are produced daily all over the world. The company has since bought out the originally leased property, and during the 19th and early 20th centuries bought most of the buildings in the surrounding area, including many streets of housing and offices for their employees.

James Joyce famously called Guinness stout "The wine of Ireland."

Left: The iconic Guinness doors showing the old train tracks once used by the brewery (FI)
Right: The brewery gates on St. James's Street (Geneviéve Murphy)

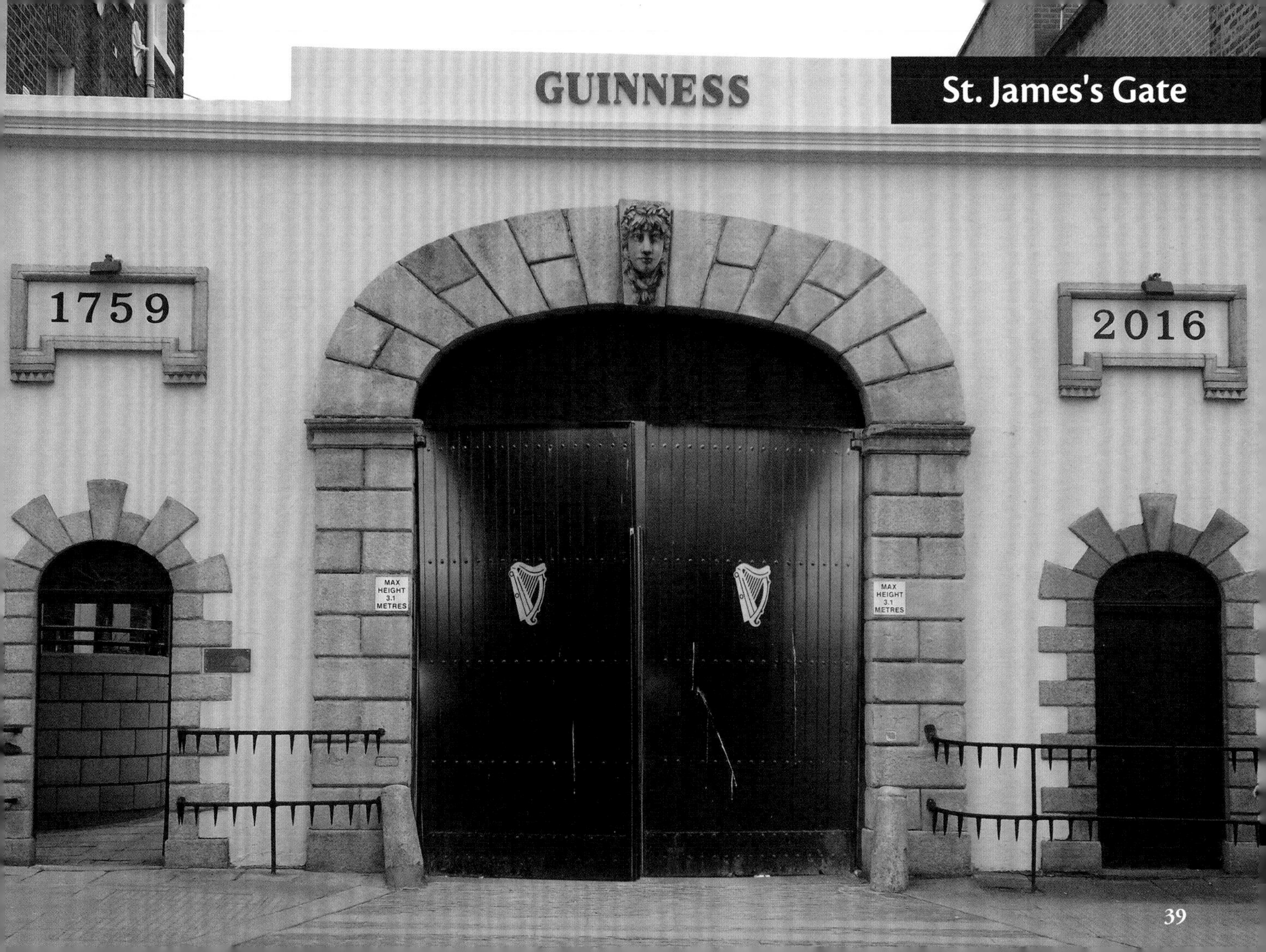

St. James's Gate

Dublin Zoo is the 2nd oldest in the world after London Zoo in Regents Park. It was opened in 1831 and covers 28 hectares (69 acres) of the Phoenix Park. When first opened it was funded by members of the medical profession (anatomists and physicists) who were interested in studying animals while they were alive and more importantly using the dead bodies for dissection. The role of the zoo today is to "work in partnership with zoos worldwide to make a significant contribution to the conservation of endangered species on Earth". There are over 400 animals on view which makes the zoo the most popular family attraction in Ireland, with more than 1 million visitors annually. Dublin Zoo is part of the European Endangered Species Programme and breeds and protects the golden lion tamarin, the Moluccan cockatoo, Rodrigues fruit bats, Goeldi's monkey and the white-tailed saki.

During the Easter Rising of 1916 food became scarce and in order to keep the lions and tigers alive some of the other animals were sacrificed.

Dublin Zoo was always world famous for its lions (see #58) and one noted celebrity visitor was U.S. President Ulysses S. Grant who included the zoo as part of his Irish tour shortly after leaving office.

Left and Right: A small selection of the different species of animals in the Zoo (FI)

The harbour at Dun Laoghaire (formerly Kingstown) is the largest man made harbour in the world. In nautical terms it is known as an asylum harbour and was built to facilitate trade ships using Dublin Port. At the time, silting of the River Liffey was still a problem and ships often had to wait days before being allowed to dock. The ships were open to storms and gales and it was decided that a safe harbour was needed. Dun Laoghaire was the most suitable location and the foundation stone for the harbour walls was laid in 1815. It took 40 years and a workforce of 600 men to finish the project, costing c. £700,000. The harbour could then boast 2 huge granite piers, the stone being quarried at nearby Dalkey and Killiney. The East pier is 1.3km (0.8ml) in length and the West Pier is 1.5 km (0.9 ml), the total area enclosed is 102 hectares (250 acres).

Left: The tranquil night-time view of the harbour (Marcus Rahm)
Right: Dun Laoghaire as seen from Killiney Hill (Thomas Mulchi)

The Dublin Electricity Generating Station, otherwise known as Pigeon House, was opened in 1903. There was great demand on power and the coal burning station has the distinction of being the first in the world to distribute three-phase electricity. This was quite controversial and risky at the time as three-phase was normally only used in the supply of power to factories and heavy load usage. The risk proved successful and Pigeon House became something of a model for electricity production internationally. The station continued to generate power until 1976 when it was superseded by the new Poolbeg Station. Pigeon House is named after John Pidgeon who was the caretaker of tools and equipment at the building of the 'South Wall' during the early 18th century. The Pigeon House site has had many roles; starting as a musical Tavern, then a Military Post and finally an electricity generating station.

Left: Interior of the power station, now derelict, was used to shoot a music video.
Right: Old Pigeon House at dusk (Sheila McNeice)

Daniel O'Connell is known in Irish History as 'The Liberator' - because he helped achieve full political rights for Catholics. A man of peace, he did not take part in the 1798 Rebellion and in 1815 was very distressed when he killed a man who had forced him into a duel. O'Connell believed that change could be achieved through political means rather than by force. In 1823 he formed the Catholic Association; his objectives were Catholic Emancipation, the right to sit in Parliament and the right to hold state and judicial posts. Membership of the Association was a penny a month. In 1828 he won a seat in the House of Commons for County Clare. He could not take his seat until George IV, fearing a rebellion in Ireland, passed the Emancipation Bill the following year. O'Connell became the first Catholic in modern history to sit in the House of Commons. He then concentrated on winning repeal of the Act of Union and establishing an Irish Parliament. Monster meetings were organised and huge crowds gathered to hear him speak.

O'Connell became the first Roman Catholic Lord Mayor of Dublin Corporation (1841-42), Dublin's O'Connell Street is named after him and he established Glasnevin Cemetery in 1828 (see #62).

Left: The Liberator with Irish wolfhound (National Library of Ireland)
Right: Daniel O'Connell monument at the top of O'Connell Street (Mel Foody)

Leinster House in Kildare Street, Dublin, is the seat of the Government of Ireland since 1922. Dáil Éireann (Irish Parliament) and the Seanad (Senate) both sit here. The house was built in 1745 for the Duke of Leinster and was the biggest private home in Dublin. At the time of its construction most of the rich and titled lived on the north-side of the city but the Duke of Leinster announced that "where he leads others follow." Thus many rich residents began to build on the south-side of the city. Leinster House has another claim to fame in that the design of the White House in Washington D.C. was based directly on it. Irish architect James Hoban won a competition to design the American Presidents House. Hoban had been working in Dublin prior to moving to America. The layout of the 1st and 2nd floors of Leinster House was used as the floor design for the White House while Leinster house itself was used as a model for the original stone-cut exterior. After the destruction of the White House in 1814 by the British forces, Hoban was retained to rebuild it and added the State and War Offices.

Left: Hoban's 1793 drawings of the White House (PD) (bottom) James Hoban architect of the White House. Waxen bas-relief on glass from the White House Historical Association (PD)
Right: (top) Leinster House, Dublin (James Stringer) (bottom) The White House, Washington DC (Michael Bell)

The Hugh Lane Gallery, officially called Dublin City Gallery, is located in Charlemont House in Parnell Square. It is the first known public gallery of modern art in the world and is home to exceptional Irish and continental paintings. It houses the collection of Impressionist paintings bequeathed by Sir Hugh Lane who made his fortune in the London art world. Unfortunately, he was on board the Lusitania when it was torpedoed off the County Cork coast in 1915. Lane's last wish was for his collection of paintings to remain in Dublin and he added a codicil to this effect. After his death, it was discovered that the codicil to his will had no witness, and his collection of paintings at the time were on loan to a London Gallery. The British refused to hand over the collection and after many years of verbal battles it was agreed that the collection would be divided and exchanged every 5 years.

A recent addition to the gallery is the reconstructed studio of the artist Francis Bacon, who was born in Baggot Street in 1909 and lived in Paris, Berlin and then in London. He died in 1992 and his heir donated the contents of his studio to the Hugh Lane Gallery. The studio at 7 Reece Mews, London was dismantled and relocated to Dublin. One of Bacon's paintings sold for over $44 million in 2012.

Left: Francis Bacon Studio (7 Reece Mews Francis Bacon Studio. Photograph: Perry Ogden Collection: Dublin City Gallery - The Hugh Lane © The Estate of Francis Bacon. All rights reserved, DACS)
Right: Exterior of the Hugh Lane Gallery
Insert: Hugh Lane (Portrait Collection - Dublin City Gallery - The Hugh Lane)

#24   *Bull Island and Mutiny on the Bounty*

Up to the year 1800, Dublin Bay had major problems with silting and a slow ebbing tide. A survey of the Bay was commissioned and a certain Captain William Bligh paid a visit to advise on the problem. This was some 10 years after his famous mutiny on the Bounty. Bligh came up with the idea of the Bull Wall which would quicken the speed of the ebbing tide and free the Bay of any obstacles, thus giving greater force to the waters entering the port. What he did not envisage was that after the completion of the wall sand and silt began to build up behind it. This in turn led to the formation of North Bull Island. The Island is now about 5km long and 800m wide and has a beach running its entire length known as Dollymount Strand.

In 1889 the Royal Dublin Golf Club, Ireland's 2nd oldest, began to lay out a golf course and construct a clubhouse on the North Bull Island. The Irish Open Championship was staged here in 1983-84-85. The Island is now one of the world's finest and most important wildlife breeding grounds – designated a National Bird Sanctuary and a UNESCO Biosphere Reserve, with a population of 180 different bird species and over 300 plants. Dollymount strand has been used as a location for movies, including *Michael Collins*, *The Van*, *D'Movie* and *Once*.

Left: North Bull Island nature reserve (William Murphy) (bottom) Captain William Bligh (PD)
Right: Aerial shot of Bull Island (Michael Foley)

The world's first pneumatic tyres were manufactured in Dublin

John Boyd Dunlop was from Scotland and was working as a vet in Dublin. He was passionate about cycling and pitied the cyclists with their wheels of solid iron, wood and rubber. When Dunlop's son started to ride his tricycle, he began to experiment with the tyres. In 1888 he invented the first practical inflatable pneumatic tyre and that same year patented the idea. The captain of the Belfast Cycling Club fitted Dunlop's tyres to his bicycle and went on to win all four cycling events at the Queen's College Sports.

Some of the local Dublin businessmen saw the potential of the invention and the following year began manufacturing a more commercial version of the tyre. They set up a workshop in Upper Stephen's Street (off the Wexford Street/Aungier Street junction). While the name Dunlop is still associated with tyre manufacturing, John Dunlop did not benefit financially from his invention.

Left: John Boyd Dunlop (PD)
Right: (top) Site of first tyre factory, cream coloured building (bottom) Plaque marking the site (David Hawgood)

Dunlop Tyres

The first pneumatic tyre factory in the world was started here in 1889, to make tyres under John Boyd Dunlop's patent of the 7th. December 1888.

The Brazen Head, Lower Bridge Street on the Liffey, is the oldest pub in Dublin and one of the oldest in Ireland. Its origins can be traced back to 1198 when a coach house was established on the site. It has served its customers from the time the Norman mercenaries and the Viking merchants traded goods and swopped slaves. At that time it was customary for the owners to provide burning buckets (or braziers) for customers and guards to warm their hands on cold nights. The name Brazen Head evolved from this custom. The pub has managed to retain the characteristics and charm of its past. The list of famous visitors past and present is very impressive, some of whom include; Jonathan Swift, Robert Emmet, Wolfe Tone, Daniel O'Connell, Michael Collins, James Joyce, Brendan Behan. And in most recent times The Dubliners, Van Morrison, Garth Brooks and many more.

Left: Wall mural of the pub
Right: Exterior of the pub maintains its old character (Jim Nix)

The 'Jeanie Johnston' (replica of a Famine Ship) is moored at Custom House Quay in Dublin. It was built in Quebec, Canada in 1847. The 408 ton cargo ship was purchased by John Donovan and Sons of Tralee, County Kerry. As the famine gripped Ireland, the company ran a successful trade bringing emigrants from Ireland to North America and returning with timbers bound for Europe. In April 1848 as the effects of the Great Famine continued to ravage Ireland, the Jeanie Johnston made her maiden voyage as an emigrant's ship. She sailed from Blennerville with 193 passengers on board. Between the years 1848 and 1855 she made 16 journeys to Quebec, New York and Baltimore. The average journey took 48-50 days and the largest number ever carried on one voyage was 254. The total number of famine emigrants carried by the Jeanie Johnston was over 2,500. No passenger or crew member ever lost their life on board the ship. This was a very remarkable achievement considering the conditions at that time and the "coffin ship" reputation of other vessels. This outstanding record is attributed to the captain, James Attridge. He never overloaded the ship, he always had adequate supplies and he had the services of a qualified doctor on board. In 1858, while transporting timber, the ship became waterlogged. The crew were all rescued and even in her sinking she maintained her unique safety record. In 2002 a replica of the Jeannie Johnston was launched and is now a museum on emigration during the Great Famine. It is open to the public at Customs House Quay to experience what our emigrants endured.

Left: Interior of the ship (Jeanie Johnston)
Right: Night time shot of 'Jeannie Johnston' moored at the quays (FI)

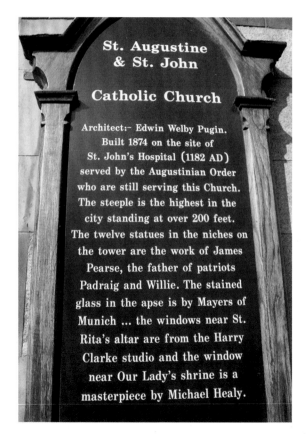

St. Augustine
& St. John

Catholic Church

Architect:– Edwin Welby Pugin.
Built 1874 on the site of
St. John's Hospital (1182 AD)
served by the Augustinian Order
who are still serving this Church.
The steeple is the highest in the
city standing at over 200 feet.
The twelve statues in the niches on
the tower are the work of James
Pearse, the father of patriots
Padraig and Willie. The stained
glass in the apse is by Mayers of
Munich ... the windows near St.
Rita's altar are from the Harry
Clarke studio and the window
near Our Lady's shrine is a
masterpiece by Michael Healy.

James Pearse, father of Padraig, was a stone mason and monument sculptor who moved from Birmingham, England to Dublin and set up business at 27 Great Brunswick Street (now called Pearse Street). The business flourished and provided the Pearse family with a comfortable middle-class upbringing. James is famous for his sculpting of the statue Éire go Brágh (Ireland forever) which sits on top of the former National Bank building in College Green, Dublin (now the Abercrombie and Fitch store). The sculpture, of Portland stone, shows 'Hibernia' with a harp, a wolfhound and symbols of prosperity. A shamrock and the slogan 'Éire go Bragh' also feature on the sculpture. A second important example of his work, a sculpture of the Twelve Apostles, can be seen on the pinnacle of the Church of St. Augustine and St. John in Thomas Street. James Pearse died in 1900 and left an estate valued at c. £1,500. The company, Pearse and Sons, was wound up in 1910 and some of the money was used to fund Padraig's school, St Enda's in Rathfarnham.

(A.I.F.) The National Bank, College Green was founded by Daniel O'Connell. Willie Pearse, brother of Padraig, was also executed for his part in the 1916 Rising.

Left: Plaque outside St. Augustine & St. John church (William Murphy)
Right: (top) Sculpture of 'Eire go Bragh' (Tadhg Connolly) (bottom) The Pearse office and residence (Paul Thompson)
Insert: James Pearse (Courtesy Pearse Museum/OPW)

27 + ECCLESIASTICAL AND **PEARSE & SONS** ARCHITECTURAL SCULPTORS + 27

Christchurch Cathedral was founded c.1030 and is Dublin's oldest Cathedral. The more formal name is The Cathedral of the Holy Trinity. It is officially claimed as the seat of both the Church of Ireland and the Catholic Archbishop of Dublin but the Catholic Archbishop uses St. Mary's in Marlborough Street as his Pro-Cathedral (acting cathedral). In the early 12th century the Patron Saint of Dublin, Laurence O'Toole, was Archbishop of the Diocese and invited the Augustinian monks to become part of the Cathedral, which they duly did. The tomb of the medieval Norman-Welsh warlord, Strongbow, is contained here. His arrival in Ireland marked the beginning of Anglo-Norman involvement in Irish history.

A visit to the crypt, the largest in Britain and Ireland, contains the oldest known secular carvings in Ireland. Also on view is a tabernacle and candlesticks from 17th century. There is a set of stocks that were used to punish offenders in the area under the authority of the cathedral. The church had the right to enforce laws in its jurisdiction – known as it's Liberty (see #100). A very strange incident happened in 2012, when the preserved heart of Laurence O'Toole (see #37) was stolen from the Cathedral and has yet to be returned. When Christchurch was renovated in the late 19th century a Dublin Whiskey Distiller, Henry Roe, financed the work and when St. Patricks was renovated Guinness covered its costs. The Dublin wit soon renamed Christchurch 'The Whiskey Chapel' and St. Patricks 'The Beer Chapel.'

Left: The Crypt under the cathedral (FI)
Right: Christchurch in all its splendour (FI)

Christchurch

Lambay Island is the largest and most isolated island off the east coast of Ireland. It lies approximately 4 km from the north Dublin coastline and has an area of 250 ha (1,300 acres). Lambay is home to an unwanted population of black rats. They arrived as stowaways on freight containers and ships. Non-native rodents such as these dramatically affect island ecosystems which tend to be small and specialized. Rats have a particular hunger for eggs and prey upon birds, reptiles and other small species. The Black Rat is blamed for bringing the great plague or Black Death to Ireland between 1348 and 1350. The disease was transmitted by the fleas the rats carried and up to half the population of many European countries died from the epidemic.

The black rat is now probably our rarest land mammal as they were completely replaced (except Lambay) when its larger, brown cousin arrived here in the 1720's. Co-existing happily on Lambay Island with the rats is a small population of Wallabies. This group was introduced to the island by Dublin Zoo after a sudden population explosion in the mid 1980s. They could not accommodate the wallabies in other zoos so they placed them on Lambay Island. The Island is privately owned by members of the Bering Family who reside on the island. Permission is required to visit Lambay.

Left: A wallaby with young joey on Lambay Island (Kevin Kirkham)
Right: The scarce black rats are still found on the island. (Wildlife Centre, Lingfield)

To many people today 'Yahoo' is a search engine for the internet. The term 'Yahoo' was first used by Jonathan Swift while writing *Gulliver's Travels*. The Yahoos were a race of fictional beings who were filthy and had very unpleasant habits. The term was thus used in the dictionary to mean: 'crude, brutish or obscenely course person'.

Jonathan Swift wrote *Gulliver's Travels* as a political satire. But children took it at face value and loved the story of the world Swift created. It has been a children's literary classic ever since and has never been out of print. Swift was born in Hoey's Court, Dublin, in 1667. As an adult he moved to England to work as a secretary, a time he did not enjoy and inspired him to write his satire.

He was Dean of St. Patricks Cathedral (see #41) from 1713 until his death in 1745 at the age of 77. His death mask, a cast of his skull and early editions of his writings are in the cathedral. Swift left money in his will to found St. Patricks Hospital for the treatment of mental illness, still in existence today.

Left: Jonathan Swift (PD)
Right: Painting of *Gullivers Travels* by Richard Redgrave (PD)
Insert: A bust of Swift in St Patricks Cathedral (PD)

Irish poet Patrick Kavanagh wrote the words to the well known song *On Raglan Road*. The road is located in Ballsbridge, Dublin and the poem is about Kavanagh's love for a young woman who lived on a 'quiet street'. The poet met up with Luke Kelly of the well-known band The Dubliners in 'The Bailey' pub. Try as they might the two failed to come up with a better matching air than the traditional Irish song *The Dawning of the Day* known in Irish as *Fáinne Geal an Lae*, written in 1847 and published by Edward Walsh. The English version *The Dawning of the Day* was published by Patrick Joyce in 1873. *On Raglan Road* became synonymous with Luke Kelly and few could master the spirit that Kelly's voice brought to this song. Some famous artists who recorded it include; Van Morrison, Sinead O'Connor, Mark Knopfler (Dire Straits), Billy Bragg, Roger Daltrey and the High Kings. Luke Kelly's version is featured in the film *In Bruges* and Andrew Scott performs the song in the Irish film *The Stag*.

Left: The Singer Luke Kelly (Brendan J. Murphy)
Right: : The Poet Patrick Kavanagh's bench beside the Grand Canal (William Murphy)
Insert: Photo of Raglan Road (Gerard Denneny)

BOTHAR RAGLAN
RAGLAN ROAD 4

County Dublin is located on the east coast of Ireland and is part of the province of Leinster. It is the 3rd smallest county in Ireland, only Carlow and Louth are smaller in size. Its area is 922 sq km (356 sq mls). The length of the county is 52 km (32 mls) from the summit of Kippure Mountain, south of the city, to the river Delvin, near Balbriggan. Its width is 27 km (16.5 mls) from Howth Head to Clonee. At 757 m (2,484 ft) the highest point is Kippure Mountain which has the boundary lines of Wicklow and Dublin passing over its summit. Counties Meath, Kildare and Wicklow all border Dublin County. It is the most populated county in Ireland with over 1,273,069 inhabitants (census 2011). Dublin City is the capital city of the Republic of Ireland and has a population of 527,612. Prior to 1994 County Dublin was administered by Dublin County Council and Dublin City Council, but with the population growth it was decided to abolish Dublin County Council and replaced with 3 separate administrative councils; Fingal County Council, Dun Laoghaire-Rathdown County Council and South Dublin County Council. Dublin City Council remains responsible for the area inside the city limits.

(A.I.F) All national distances to and from Dublin are measured from the General Post Office (GPO).

Left: Views from the Dublin mountains (FI)
Right: The location of Dublin on the map of Ireland
Insert: The four administrative councils of County Dublin (David Murphy)

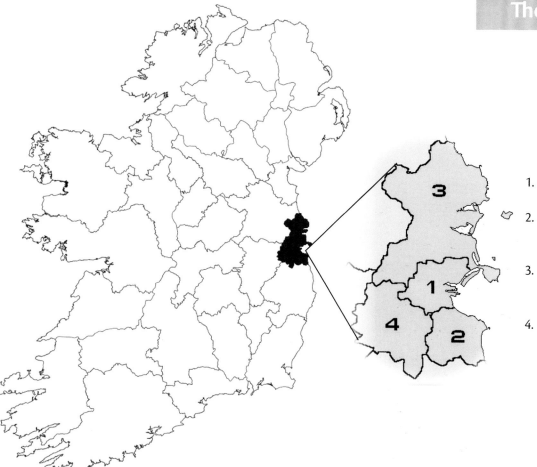

1. Dublin City Council

2. Dun Laoghaire – Rathdown

3. Fingal County Council

4. South Dublin

Arthur Shields in "The New Gossoon"

Arthur Shields (1896 – 1970) born in Portobello, Dublin, was part of an interesting twist of fate. During the 1916 Easter Rising Shields was a volunteer and was stationed in O'Connell Street. Because of overwhelming odds he and his comrades had to abandon their position and retreat to Moore Street where their Commanding Officer, Padraig Pearse, had to surrender. Shields was captured and interned in Frongoch Camp, Wales along with Michael Collins and Arthur Griffith. Some years after his release he moved to the USA and continued with his other passion, acting.

In 1941 Shields was cast in the movie *How Green was My Valley.* One of his co-stars was John Loder (1898-1988) who was born William John Lowe. Lowe was in Dublin during the 1916 Easter Rising, a serving officer in the British Army he was on leave from the World War I trenches and visiting his father General Lowe. When Padraig Pearse surrendered, the arresting officer was this same General Lowe. In the photo (top right) the officer in the white trousers is John Lowe (Loder).

(A.I.F) Arthur Shields had a famous brother, William Joseph Shields, better known by his stage name, Barry Fitzgerald (1888-1961).

Left: Arthur Shields (National Library of Ireland)
Right: (top) John Lowe (John Loder) in white trousers at the surrender of Pearse (National Library of Ireland) (bottom) Slide from the film *How Green was My Valley* (PD)
Extreme Right: John Loder with actress Hedy Lamarr (PD)

"w Green Was my Valley" 20th Century Fox Production

Cast: *Walter Pidgeon, Maureen O'Hara, Anna Lee, Donald Crisp, Roddy McDowall, Sara Allgood, Barry Fitzgerald, Patric Knowles, Evan S. Evans, James Monks, Arthur Shields, John Loder, Rhys Williams, Richard Fraser. Directed by John Ford.*

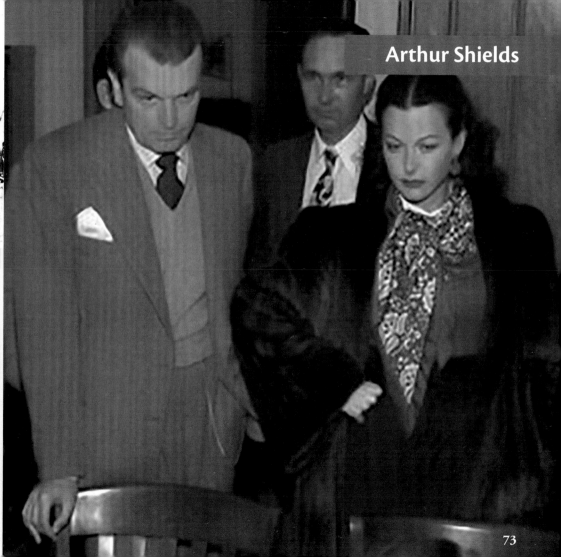

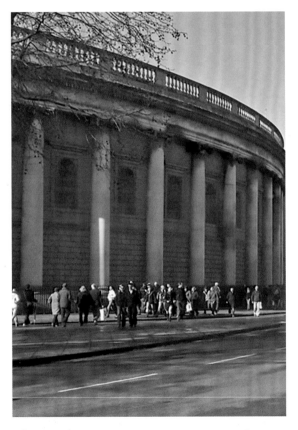

The Bank of Ireland building, directly across from Trinity College, was designed by Sir Edward Lovett Pearse and was originally built for the Irish Parliament in 1728. It was the first purpose built parliament building in the world. The Irish Parliament governed from here until 1800 when it voted itself out of existence – the only recorded parliament to do so. The Act of Union was passed which merged the Irish and British Parliament and was seated in Westminster, London. The building was taken over by the Bank of Ireland in 1803 and has remained a bank ever since.

The building was erected without windows. The term "daylight robbery" was coined during a period of time when there was a tax on glass. Therefore many buildings were erected without windows to save on the taxes. Citizens of the country complained that the Government was now even robbing them of their daylight.

Left: Close up of bank building with windows blocked up (William Murphy)
Right: Bank of Ireland building College Green (William Murphy)

Balbriggan in North County Dublin was the location of Smyth's Stocking Mill. The Mill was one of the largest manufacturers of ladies stockings and men's underwear. It opened in 1780 and continued production until its closure in 1980. The factory was the main provider of employment in the area. The men's 'Long John's' were knitted unbleached cotton fabric underwear; also useful was the flap at the back. In fact the 'Long John's' became known as 'Balbriggans.' They are often mentioned in John Wayne movies where he says "I'm putting on my balbriggans". Their ladies stockings were fashionably worn by society ladies as well as Queen Victoria and Czarina of Russia.

Plaques commemorating the prizes won by the Mill can still be seen high on the outside walls of the factory. The company is famous for being the second longest member of the Dublin Stock Exchange, the oldest being Guinness.

Left: Long Johns or Balbriggans (PD)
Right: Smyths factory showing awards won (William Murphy)
Insert: The Smyth factory crest (William Murphy)

LONDON
DUBLIN
&
NEWCASTLE

PARIS
PRIZE MEDAL
1867

DUBLIN
PRIZE MEDAL
1865

ESTD 1780
ORIGINAL SMYTHS HOSIERS
BALBRIGGAN
IRELAND

St. Laurence O'Toole (Lorcán Ua Tuathail) is one of two official patron saints of Dublin, the other being St. Kevin of Glendalough. St. Laurence (1128-1180) has his official feast day on 14th November. In 1161 he became the first Irish born Archbishop of Dublin, his consecration as Archbishop signalling the end of Danish supremacy in Dublin's religious circles. He was especially generous and fed the poor of the city daily in his own home. He also set up care centres for children abandoned or orphaned. He was responsible for re-building Christchurch (see #29) and several new parish churches. In 1180 he travelled to France and landed at Le Tréport, Normandy and the cove where he landed is named after him - Saint-Laurence. During this trip he fell ill and was brought to the Abbey of St. Victor at Eu, where he died on 14th November 1180. His bones were interred in St. Laurence's church in Chorley, England but disappeared after the Reformation. His heart was preserved and brought back to Christchurch where it was revered until it was mysteriously stolen in 2012 and to this day its location remains unknown. St. Laurence was canonised in 1225 by Pope Honorius III after reports of miracles by pilgrims to his tomb.

Left: Stained-glass window of St. Laurence O'Toole in Christchurch Cathedral (John James Connolly)
Right: Photo of Laurence O'Toole's heart in the cage (Stephen Barlett Travels)
Far Right: The heart is stolen (Josh Thompson)

Laurence O'Toole

William Rowan Hamilton (1805–1865) was born in Dominick Street, Dublin. He was a child prodigy who could work out mathematical calculations at a very early age and was fluent in Hebrew, Greek and Latin by the age of 14. He studied Maths at Trinity College, Dublin and at the age of 22 was made director of Dunsink Observatory (see # 64). In 1848 Hamilton had a eureka moment that would make him famous in the world of mathematics. He was walking beside the Royal Canal (see # 85) pondering a maths problem when the answer came to him. He took out his pen knife and carved the formula "$i^2 = j^2 = k^2 = ijk = -1$" on nearby Broombridge.

The formula, known as Quaternions (the first non-commutative algebra), is still in everyday use for computer graphics and manoeuvring spacecraft. There is a plaque on the bridge to mark this great moment. For his contribution to science William Rowan Hamilton has a crater on the moon named after him.

Left: Plaque on the bridge (Matthew Petroff)
Right: Broombridge where Hamilton carved his formula (Matthew Petroff)
Insert: William Rowan Hamilton (PD)

Dublin City boasts 3 branches of the National Museum of Ireland. The Kildare Street museum, opened in 1890, contains the Archaeology section. Europe's largest exhibition of Bronze Age gold jewellery is housed here, including the Tara Brooch and the Cross of Cong. The abstract designs and superb craftsmanship date from 2200 BC. Excellent samples of the treasures found in Dublin include; Gold Band and Bronze Necklet on Lambay Island, Silver Penannular Brooch in Kilmainham and Gold Rings on Arran Quay. The Prehistoric section contains artefacts from the earliest habitation in Ireland, some stone implements date back to 7,000 BC. The Battle of Clontarf (see #81) exhibition is also here.

Dublin's second branch The Natural History Museum, better known to Dubliners as 'The Dead Zoo' opened in 1857. It has over 10,000 exhibits - one of the world's largest collections of deceased animals and insects. Only a fraction of the 2 million specimens collected are on display – some are now endangered or extinct. Irish mammals and birds are all featured and include skeletons of the giant Irish Elk. The National Museum of Decorative Arts and History is located in Collins Barracks, named after the Irish Patriot Michael Collins. While the barracks is over 300 years old, the museum opened in the 1990's. The barracks is believed to have been the longest serving army base in the world and the parade ground is the largest in Ireland. The collection here includes weaponry, textiles, uniforms and furniture. Special exhibits chart the Easter Rising 1916 and the Civil War era.

Left: Gold artefacts in the National Museum (FI and the National Museum)
Right: Entrance to the Archaeology Museum, Kildare Street

George Frederick Handel (1685 - 1759) was born in Germany and was a world famous composer of operas, oratorios, anthems and organ concertos. Handel left London for Dublin in 1741 in search of a more appreciative audience for his music. Having performed a series of concerts in Dublin, he decided to host a charity concert with the intention of showcasing his new work, *The Messiah.* He was given permission to use the choirs of both St. Patrick's and Christchurch Cathedrals for the occasion. In 1742, the Music Hall in Fishamble Street hosted the very first performance of the oratorio that eventually became one of the best-known and most frequently performed choral works in Western music – *The Messiah.* The crowd was so large that the men had to leave their swords outside the hall and the ladies were asked not to wear hoops in their dresses. The charities that benefitted from the proceeds were: prisoners' debt relief, the Mercer's Hospital and the Rotunda Hospital (see #16). It is believed that Handel practised for *The Messiah* on the organ in St. Michan's Church (see #87).

Left: George Frederick Handel (PD)
Right: Handel's great work is now celebrated annually (William Murphy)
Insert: Plaque to commemorate the "Messiah" (Stephen Roden)

GEORGE FREDERIC HANDEL

Handel's Messiah

THIS BRONZE COMMEMORATES THE FIRST PERFORMANCE OF GEORGE FRIDERIC HANDEL'S ORATORIO MESSIAH, GIVEN IN THE OLD MUSICK HALL IN FISHAMBLE STREET AT NOON ON TUESDAY APRIL 13TH 1742

Saint Patrick's Cathedral was founded in 1191 and is the largest Church in Ireland. It is the National Cathedral of the Church of Ireland (Anglican community). It is not the seat of a bishop – that honour falls to Christchurch. The Cathedral was built to honour St. Patrick, Ireland's patron saint and stands adjacent to a well which is said to have been where St. Patrick baptised converts during his visit to Dublin. The present building dates from 1220 and received Cathedral status in 1224. After the Reformation in England, St. Patrick's became Anglican. When Oliver Cromwell and his soldiers were conquering Ireland, Cromwell stabled his horses in the nave of the cathedral and his soldiers defaced many images within the church. This demonstrated their disrespect for the Anglican religion. In the late 1800's the church fell into disrepair but was handed a lifeline by Benjamin Lee Guinness who spent over £150,000 on the restoration of the building. Throughout its history St. Patricks has contributed much to Dublin life; including Jonathan Swift (see #31) who was Dean of the Cathedral. His grave and epitaph are located in the church as is the Door of Reconciliation (see #11). The choir of St. Patricks is world famous and its members are still educated in the Choir School (the only one of its kind in the country).

Left: St. Patricks Cathedral (FI)
Right: Interior of Cathedral (Stephen Roden)

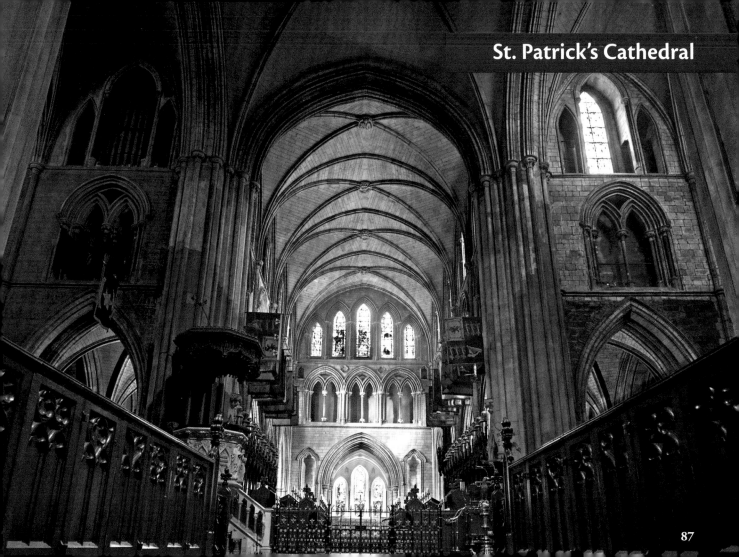

King Oscar 1 of Sweden was visiting London when he developed a serious ear infection. A famous ear and eye surgeon, William Wilde, was called upon to attend to the king. When the treatment was completed, Dr. Wilde asked that in lieu of payment for his services, he might be given permission to name his son after the king. Oscar Fingal O'Flahertie Willis Wilde (1854 – 1900) was born at 21 Westland Row, Dublin to Dr. William and Jane Wilde. Home schooled, he was taught French and German and had a working knowledge of Italian and Greek. He became a playwright, novelist, essayist, and poet. He married Constance Lloyd in 1884 and they had two sons, Vyvyan and Cyril. He published only one novel *The Portrait of Dorian Gray*, he did however write a collection of children's stories *The Happy Prince and other Tales,* still popular with children today.

In 1895, Oscar Wilde prosecuted the Marquess of Queensbury for libel. Queensbury, the father of Wilde's lover Lord Alfred Douglas, counter-sued. Wilde lost the case and was sentenced to two years hard labour. After his release he went to France, never to return, where he died in poverty and loneliness and is interred in the Père Lachaise Cemetery in Paris.

(A.I.F.) The Marguess of Queensbury is the same man who gave his name to the rules of boxing.

Jane Wilde, Oscar's mother was a poet and collector of Irish Folktales. She wrote under the pen name 'Speranza.'

Left: Statue of Oscar Wilde in Merrion Square (FI)
Right: Oscar Wilde in pensive mood (PD)

Oscar Wilde

The hilltop village of Glencullen, situated on top of the Dublin Mountains, lays claim to one of Ireland's oldest traditional pubs – Johnnie Fox's. At 276 m (906 ft) it is famed as the highest pub in Ireland. It was established in the same year as the Irish Rebellion of 1798 and was "a safe meeting venue" for Daniel O'Connell when he lived in Glencullen. Indeed his daughter Ellen married into the Fitzsimons family who have lived in the area for generations. The pub was originally part of a small family holding and areas within the bar still hold their original name; 'the haggard' and 'the pig house'. The road leading past the pub is part of the 'Wicklow Way' walking route and the 'Glencullen Cycle Loop.' Johnnie's provides 'Irish Traditional Nights' and visiting musicians are encouraged to join the *Séisiún.* The pub has provided hospitality for several heads of state and prime ministers, members of the Kennedy Family, along with celebrities including Meryl Streep, Brad Pitt, Julia Roberts, Rock Hudson, Angelina Jolie and Jack Nicholson. There are no televisions on the premises, as the owners believe "TV's in pubs have killed the art of conversation."

Left: Interior of the pub
Right: Night-time shot of the exterior (Marcin Tarkowski)

A painting with an extraordinary story is the *Taking of Christ* (1602) by Caravaggio (1571-1610). This priceless piece was found in the Jesuit House of Studies in Leeson Street, Dublin. When the Jesuit house was being renovated in the 1990's the Order decided to clean up the paintings that hung on the walls and called in Sergio Benedetti, an expert from the National Gallery. The large dark painting that hung in the dining room was of particular interest and when the thick layers of varnish and soot were cleaned off the picture, Benedetti knew he had something special. Caravaggio experts verified that it was an original. The Jesuits have allowed this painting to be exhibited in the National Gallery.

The National Art Gallery is located in the centre of Dublin beside Leinster House. The Gallery houses about 3,000 paintings and some 13,000 other works including drawings, prints and sculptures. The earliest piece dates back to the 13th century. Every major European School of Art is represented, some of the paintings are world renowned masterpieces with such recognisable names as: Monet, Picasso, Rembrandt and Van Gogh.

There is a renowned collection of Irish paintings on display and a Yeats museum with works by Jack B. Yeats and his father John (see #66). Ireland's favourite painting is also on display: Hellelil and Hildebrand, *The Meeting on the Turret Stairs* by Frederic William Burton (1816-1900).

Left: Irelands favourite painting *The Meeting on the Turret Stairs*, 1864 by Frederic William Burton (National Gallery of Ireland)
Right: *Taking of Christ* (1602) by Caravaggio (© National Gallery of Ireland By kind permission of the Jesuit Community, Leeson St. Dublin who acknowledge the kind generosity of the late Dr. Marie Lea-Wilson)

Howth Head is a rocky headland of wild, natural beauty that supports a collection of wildflowers and gorse. Fingal County Council has designated the heath-lands and coastline of the Howth Peninsula as a Special Amenity Area due to some of the more notable flora here being threatened by extinction. Many of these plants are localised and are not found in other areas of Ireland. The Green-winged Orchid (Anacamptis Morio) is one such example and is legally protected under the European Union (E.U.) Habitat Directive. It flowers from late April to June thriving on the limestone rich soil of Howth and can reach a height of 40 cm (16 ins). It is mainly purple in colour but can range from white, through pink to the deep purple colour and has anything from 5 to 25 helmet-shaped flowers at the top of the stalk.

Left: Howth Head (FI)
Right: Green-winged Orchid (Anacamptis Morio) (John Crellin)

Endangered Orchid

95

Cream Crackers are a flat savoury biscuit. They are made from wheat flour, palm oil and yeast. They are commonly served with cheese or other savoury topping. The name 'cream cracker' comes from the way the mixture is creamed during manufacture. The biscuit is produced from yeast dough that is left to ferment for 24 hours, it is then flattened and folded many times to create a layered biscuit. The cream cracker was invented by Dublin man Joseph Haughton in 1885. They were then manufactured commercially by William and Robert Jacob (W & R Jacob) of Bishop Street and Peters Row in Dublin. Cream crackers have a place in the Guinness Book of Records as being the hardest biscuit to eat quickly. The fastest time officially recorded to eat 3 cream crackers, without the aid of water is 34.78 seconds. An average cracker contains about 35 kcal. Cream crackers are now manufactured at a rate of over 1 million per hour and are available to buy in over 35 countries worldwide.

Left: Cream of Crackers (Valeo Foods)
Right: Jacob's Factory (National Library of Ireland)
Insert: Only the packaging has changed throughout the years (Valeo Foods)

JACOB'S SHEETS OF DOUGH INTO BISCUITS

In the early 13th century the Lord Mayor of Dublin ordered that all fever houses, pest houses and especially leprosy houses be built outside the city walls. One such downtrodden colony existed beside the Grand Canal Docks and was known as Misery Hill. The people lived here in squalor and in very harsh conditions and the only acceptable way to exit the quarantine was to perish. In the Medieval Ages it was widely believed that the people living in Misery Hill were going through a Purgatory on Earth. The medical belief was that leprosy was contagious so those who contracted the disease had to move outside the walls. The 'unclean' walked silently behind a man tolling a bell, accompanied by Beadles, who were minders appointed by the Lord Mayor. The Beadles carried 40 foot white poles to keep everyone at a safe distance. From this practice we get the expression "I wouldn't touch him with a forty foot pole." St. Stephen's Hospital (now Mercers Hospital) was an ancient site for lepers and the name Leopardstown derived from another colony in that area.

Left: Misery Hill in the modern docklands (Cashen)
Right: Leprosy victims as depicted by Harry Clarke Studio in Saint Peter & Pauls Church Balbriggan (Aidan McRae Thompson)

#48   *A Half-penny to cross the bridge*

The Ha'penny Bridge at Temple Bar is so called because it originally cost half a penny to cross. Before it was built a ferry crossed between the two banks transporting people from the north side to the south side. The toll was introduced following the construction of a new arch bridge in 1816 as the owner of the ferry had to be compensated. William Walsh, also a city alderman, duly retired his creaking ferries and was given a lease on the bridge for 100 years. People were charged the toll for crossing the Liffey up until 1919. Originally it was called the Wellington Bridge (after the Duke of Wellington see #80). Its official name now is the Liffey Bridge, although it is still commonly referred to as the Ha'penny Bridge. It is the oldest Iron Bridge in Ireland and one of the oldest cast-iron bridges in the world.

Left and Right: The Ha'penny bridge an icon of the city (FI)
Insert: The ha'penny coin (PD)

Ha' penny Bridge

Dublin's newest landmark is the Spire of Dublin, which soars above O'Connell Street in front of the General Post Office. Unveiled on 21 January 2003, it is made of stainless steel and at 121.2 metres (398 ft) in height is the tallest sculpture in the world. It replaced Nelson's Pillar and is officially called 'The Monument of Light' but is affectionately known locally as 'The Stiletto in the Ghetto.'

Nelson's Pillar was erected in 1808 and during its time on O'Connell Street was part of a time-line that included; Catholic Emancipation, the Great Famine, the Land War, the Gaelic Revival, the Easter Rising, the Troubles and the visit of President John F. Kennedy in 1963. The pillar, erected in memory of Horatio Nelson, was 41m (134 ft.) high and enclosed a spiral staircase giving access to a viewing platform. However, in 1966, the 50th anniversary of the Easter Rising, it was destroyed by a bomb planted by Irish Republicans. The head from Nelson's Pillar was retrieved and can be seen at an exhibition in Dublin's Civic Museum.

Left: Nelsons Pillar (National Library)
Right: Sunset shot of The Spire as it towers over O'Connell Street (Dreamstime)

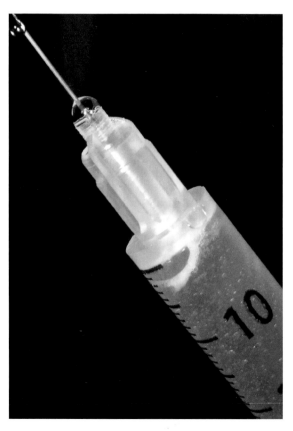

Dr. Francis Rynd (1801-61) was working at the Meath Hospital in Heytesbury Street and in 1844 was treating a woman who had suffered constant pain in her face for many years. Although she was taking morphine tablets they were giving no relief. Dr. Rynd decided to place the morphine directly under her skin, near the nerves. He made an improvised syringe out of tubing, which allowed the morphine flow through the tubing and into place under the skin. This was the first time the procedure was ever attempted and it led to the commonly used hypodermic syringe. Nearly 15 billion hypodermic syringes are now used every year.

Left: Syringe and needle (PD)
Right: The Meath Hospital (PD)
Far Right: Hypodermic needles (PD)

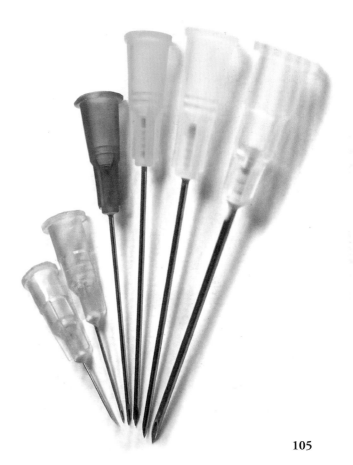

Brendan Gleeson came to prominence in *Braveheart*. His other major roles include; *Turbulence, The General* and *Mission Impossible II*. These were followed by *The Tailor of Panama* and *Gangs of New York*. Gleeson played the part of Hogwarts professor, Mad-Eye Moody in the Harry Potter films. His most recent films include; *The Guard, Calvary* and *Assassins Creed*. He is a fluent Irish speaker and plays the fiddle and mandolin.

Colm Meaney, who starred in 216 episodes of *Star Trek*, was born in Finglas. He took the leading role in Roddy Doyle's *The Barrytown Trilogy*. His movies tended to have hijacking plots including *Die Hard 2, Under Siege* and *Con Air*. He starred in *Law Abiding Citizen* and had a major role in the blockbuster television series *Hell on Wheels*.

Colin Farrell was born in Castleknock. He auditioned for Irish Boy band, Boyzone and his acting career began in *Ballykissangel*. Farrell went on to star in *American Outlaws* and *Hart's War*. In 2002 he was cast in *Minority Report* and *Phone Booth*. Farrell's most infamous role was in *Alexander*. Recent work includes *Saving Mr. Banks, Winters Tale* and *True Detective*.

Gabriel Byrne was born in Walkinstown and began his career in Irish Television. He made his film debut in *Excalibur*. He has now starred in over 50 movies including; *Miller's Crossing, Into the West, The Usual Suspects, Stigmata, End of Days* and *Spider*. He was Executive Producer of *In The Name of the Father* and starred in the T.V. series *Vikings* and *In Treatment* (Golden Globe Award). He is a UNICEF Ireland Ambassador.

Left: Brendan Gleeson (Dreamstime)
Right: Colm Meaney **Centre:** Gabriel Byrne **Far Right:** Colin Farrell (All Shutterstock)

In 2004 UNESCO set up the Creative Cities network. City of Literature is one of seven designations for which a city may apply. The others are Music, Gastronomy, Design, Film, Folk Art and Media Art. The application process is an onerous one and the success rate is quite low. The aim of UNESCO is to "promote the social, economic and cultural development of cities in both the developed world and developing worlds". In 2010 Dublin was chosen as the City of Literature and this is a permanent designation. Dublin's claim to literary excellence can never be questioned – many judge this on the writers of the past and this list reads like a 'who's who' in the literary world – Joyce, Behan, Yeats, Swift, Beckett, Shaw, Wilde, Stoker, Le Fanu, Plunkett and Pearse, but the literary talents of 21st century Dublin writers must also be acknowledged. Maeve Binchy's talent as a novelist, playwright and short story writer made her one of Ireland's best-loved and most recognised writers. Her novels were translated into 38 languages and sold more than 40 million copies. Roddy Doyle is a novelist, dramatist and screenwriter who has written novels for adults and children. Several of his books have been made into films, *The Commitments* in 1991 being the most famous. He was the Man Booker Prize winner in 1993. While Anne Enright's novel *The Gathering* won the 2007 Man Booker Prize. Emma Donoghue's 2010 novel *Room* was adapted into a film and won an Academy Award. Author Lee Dunne is best known for his novel *Goodbye to the Hill*. In 1976 his novel *Midnight Cabbie* was the last piece of literature to be banned in Ireland by the Censorship of Publications Board.

Left & Right: UNESCO – Dublin City of Literature brand and logo (Dublin City Libraries)

Joseph Murphy worked from his small premises on O'Rahilly Parade off Moore Street in Dublin. He produced potato crisps for the city residents. However, in 1954 Joseph 'Spud' Murphy began to experiment with different flavourings for his crisps and developed a cheese and onion variety that was a success at home and abroad. His company Tayto had initial set up costs of £500 and his entire staff consisted of eight employees and a single delivery van. The brand name Tayto came about courtesy of Murphy's eldest son Joseph. He was unable to pronounce 'potato', calling them 'tatos' and with the addition of a 'y' – the Tayto brand was born. A bag of crisps was then selling for 4d (old pennies) a bag and the crisp bags were hand-glued with tiny paintbrushes to guarantee the freshness. The range was expanded to include other flavours, the salt and vinegar variety was the next most popular. In 1954 Tayto were selling 350 packs per day, today it sells 525 packs a minute. Tayto is still the number 1 crisps and snacks brand in Ireland. In 1999 Tayto was acquired by Irish company C&C plc. and in 2006 Largo Foods bought the company. In 2010, a new theme park called "Tayto Park" was opened near Ashbourne, County Meath and it boasts the largest wooden roller coaster with an inversion in Europe.

Left: The official opening of the Tayto factory in 1968 (Joe "Spud" Murphy with Minister George Colley, Allan W. Adams and Taoiseach Sean Lemass)
Right: Tayto pack today **Centre:** The original tin Tayto packs were sold in.
Far Right: The 1st Tayto pack (Largo Foods)

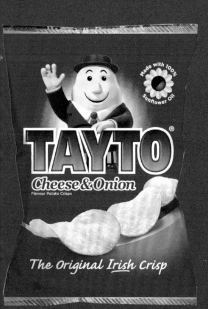

The Chester Beatty Library has been described as not just the best museum in Ireland but one of the best in Europe and has the distinction of winning the 'European Museum of the Year' (2002). It was established in Dublin in 1950 and moved to its present location in Dublin Castle in 2000. The Library houses a rich collection of artistic treasures of the great cultures and religions of Asia, Middle East, North Africa and Europe. There are beautifully illuminated copies of the Qur'an, Egyptian papyrus texts, the Bible, medieval and renaissance manuscripts, the oldest dating back to 2700 BC. The artefacts include; paintings, manuscripts, drawings, prints, rare books and decorative art. The collection is so unique and rare that some visitors have been known to weep openly when they view the displays. Earliest known copies of the Four Gospels and the Acts of the Apostles, dating from the second to the fourth century, are on display. The benefactor, Alfred Chester Beatty (1875-1968), was a very rich Irish-American copper mining magnate. He was born in New York and was made an honorary citizen of Ireland in 1957. Because of his generous donations to the State he was given a State Funeral in 1968 – one of the few private citizens to be so honoured.

Left & Right: The unique collections of religious manuscripts and decorative art are beautifully displayed in the Library (Chester Beatty Library)

The Dublin Hurling Club was formed in 1882, and Michael Cusack, a founding member of the Gaelic Athletic Association (G.A.A.), played a prominent role. His involvement was 'for the purpose of taking steps to re-establish the national game of hurling'. After the formation of the G.A.A in 1884, Dublin teams took part in both hurling and football championships.

Dublin hurlers achieved All-Ireland success in 1889 – 2 years before the footballers claimed their first title. They have played in 21 finals - winning 6. Their last winning title was in 1938. The hurling squad have won the National Hurling League in 1929, 1939 and recently in 2011.

Dublin footballers won their first All-Ireland title in 1891. To date they have won 25 senior titles – only Kerry with 37 have won more than Dublin. Dublin have played in 38 All-Ireland Football finals and were the first team to play in a record 6 in-a-row between 1974 and 1979. They have won the National Football League on 13 occasions. In the Ladies games, Dublin won 26 camogie All-Ireland titles, while the footballers won a title in 2010.

Left: Dublin Hurlers in action V's Galway
Right: All-Ireland Senior Football winners after defeating Kerry 2015 (County Dublin GAA Board)

Robert Collis (1900-75) was a Dublin Doctor who practiced at the Rotunda Hospital (see #16). He pioneered a technique to feed premature babies via a nasal tube to the stomach and the survival rate increased dramatically by this method. He also designed a simple but affordable incubator for premature babies – less well-off hospitals could then afford the machines. Dr Collis worked for a time with the Red Cross in the German concentration camps where he witnessed some horrific living conditions. On his return to Dublin he helped set up Cerebral Palsy Ireland. One of his patients was Christy Brown (1932-81) who was born in the Rotunda Hospital into a large working-class family of 22 children. Doctors discovered that he had severe cerebral palsy and urged the family to commit him to a hospital. His parents would not consider it and reared him with the rest of the family in Kimmage. Though Christy could only type with the toes of his left foot that did not stop him from writing. Doctor Collis recognised his talent and used his connections to get his book *My Left Foot* published. Dublin film director Jim Sheridan adapted the book into a film of the same title. Both Brenda Fricker and Daniel Day Lewis received Oscars (see #6) for their roles.

Left: Christy Brown working on his typewriter as his young nephew Darren looks on (National Library of Ireland)
Right: Dr. Collis developed cost efficient incubators (Shutterstock)
Insert: Dr. Robert Collis friend of Christy and pioneer of studies of premature babies (National Library of Ireland)

The Dublin Transport Strike, also known as 'The Great Dublin Lockout,' began on 26th August 1913. It was led by Jim Larkin and James Connolly. Jim Larkin wanted to unionise workers to achieve better conditions for employees, such as the eight-hour day, pensions at 60 and the nationalisation of public transport. He founded the Irish Trade and General Workers' Union in 1909. He coined the phrase "A fair days work for a fair days pay." The lockout lasted nearly 8 months and affected tens of thousands of Dublin's workers. The strike was a failure but eventually the workers achieved better pay and conditions. There is a statue in memory of 'Big Jim' in O'Connell Street, Dublin. An inscription on the front of the monument is an extract in French, Irish and English from one of his famous speeches "The great appear great because we are on our knees: Let us rise." Songs, poems and plays have also been written about him. The Transport and General Workers Union of America took its name in tribute to Larkin and the Irish Union.

Left: Plaque with famous quote by Jim Larkin (Michelle O'Connell Photography)
Right: 'Big Jim' statue near the GPO (FI)
Insert: Jim Larkin is arrested during 'the lockout' (National Library of Ireland)

The fearsome lion that roars at the beginning and end of early Metro Goldwyn Meyer films is one of the most recognisable shots from the movies. The original lion used in the scene was born in Dublin Zoo in 1919 (see #18). This lion, called Slats, was used on all MGM films from 1924 to 1928. When he was born, the lion was given the name Cairbre, a popular medieval Irish name borne by several historical and mythological figures. The Zoo decided to sell him and the new owners changed his name to Slats as they had difficulty pronouncing Cairbre. The first MGM film that used the lion logo was *He Who Gets Slapped* (1924). In his first few movies Slats did nothing but look around in the logo and was therefore the only MGM lion not to roar. He was later trained to roar on cue by Volney Phifer, Hollywood's premier animal trainer. Slats then toured the world to promote MGM's launch. He died in 1936 and his story is told in detail at the McPherson Museum in Kansas U.S.A.

Left: Original MGM logo with Slats the lion (PD)
Right: Recording the lions roar for the talking movies (PD)

#59   *The Garden with 300 Endangered Species*

The National Botanic Gardens (Irish: Garraithe Náisiúnta na Lus) are located in Glasnevin. The area of the garden is 19.5 hectares (48 acres) and it contains over 20,000 plant species from habitats all over the world. It is home to 300 endangered plant species including 6 already extinct in the wild. Founded in 1795 by the Royal Dublin Society (R.D.S.) it opened to the public in 1800. The garden has excellent displays of herbaceous borders, rose gardens, an alpine yard, a pond area, rock gardens and an arboretum. It serves as a centre of horticultural research and is famous for its breeding of prize winning orchids. The glasshouses have received the Europa Nostra award for excellence in conservation architecture. The Great Palm House measures 20m (65 ft) in height, 30.5m (100ft) in length and 24m (80ft) wide. It was built in 1862 to accommodate plants from tropical areas. The Curvilinear Range glasshouse was completed in 1848 and had to be extended in the 1860's, it is now 91.5m (300ft) long with various wings and extensions to the sides. It is the most important building on site and its central dome was featured on Irish stamps. The National Herbarium is also based in the garden and has a collection of nearly ¾ million dried plant specimens. In 1845 staff at the gardens identified the fungus infection responsible for the Great Famine (1845-52) but sadly they narrowly missed out finding a remedy to kill the fungus.

Left: Inside the Palm House
Right: (top) The planned lay-out of the gardens (bottom) The Curvilinear Range of glasshouses (William Murphy)

In April 1994 the Eurovision Song Contest was being held in the Point Depot (see #76). The piece that stole the show was the interval act of traditional Irish music and dance, lasting all of 7 minutes. The performance received a standing ovation and was named the most popular interval act in the history of the competition. John McColgan and Moya Doherty, along with music composer Bill Whelan, expanded it into a full length stage show, adding its own orchestra, singers and a full Irish Dance Troupe. World Irish dancing champions Michael Flatley and Jean Butler were the original lead dancers. *Riverdance* then went on to become an internationally celebrated music and dance phenomenon, seen by several heads of state. It has played at over 350 venues worldwide in 30 different countries and has been seen by over 25 million people. It has shattered box office records and has been viewed by a worldwide audience exceeding 3 billion. This global sensation has several different *Riverdance* productions touring at any one time, each named after an Irish river, to date they include Shannon, Avoca, Boyne, Liffey and Moy. The troupe has had over 2,000 Irish dancers and the companies have travelled over 700,000 miles (to the moon and back and back again). In 2008 they danced on the Great Wall of China and the following year embarked on a sold out tour of China.

Left: Scene from *Riverdance*
Right: The finale of the show (*Riverdance* production photos by kind permission of Abhann Productions)

#61　*Erotic Female Vampires Began in Chapelizod*

Joseph Sheridan Le Fanu (1814-1873) was born in Dominick Street, Dublin. He studied law in Trinity College, Dublin but never practised, preferring instead the discipline of journalism. Le Fanu's early life and education was in Chapelizod and the Phoenix Park area of Dublin, areas that would later feature as settings for his writings. Le Fanu was the leading ghost-story writer of the 19th century and is best remembered for mystery and horror-fiction. His most terrifying tale was *Carmilla*, a chilling vampire story with lesbian undertones. It is widely believed that this book greatly influenced Bram Stoker in his writing of *Dracula* (see #1). *Carmilla* spawned many works of vampire fiction and was made into a movie titled *The Vampire Lovers* starring Ingrid Pitt and Peter Cushing.

Other famous titles by this author include *Uncle Silas* and *The House by the Churchyard*; the latter novel had an important influence on James Joyce's *Finnegans Wake* and is set in Chapelizod. The house that inspired the novel still stands beside the village church. A road and a park in Ballyfermot are named after Le Fanu.

Left: Sheridan Le Fanu (PD)
Right: The seductive vampire Carmilla attacks a sleeping victim (PD)
Insert: Carmilla watches the funeral of a victim (PD)

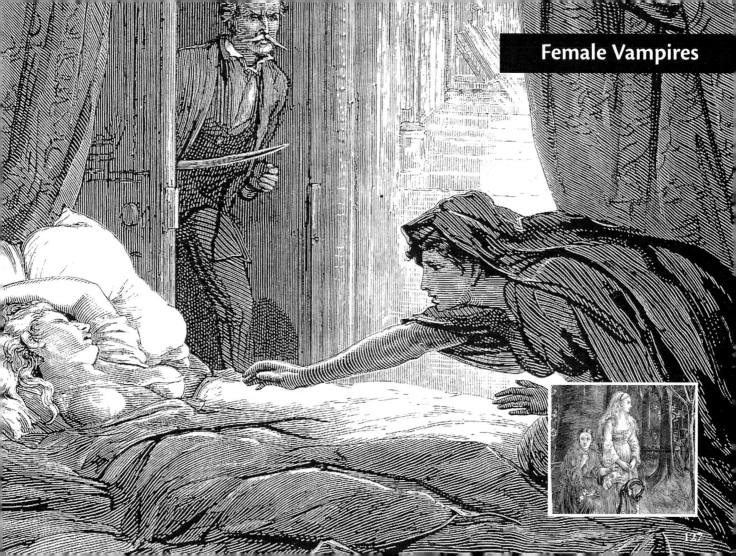

125

Originally called Prospect Cemetery, renamed Glasnevin, is Ireland's largest cemetery which was opened in 1828. It was established by Daniel O'Connell as a place where people of 'all religions and none' could bury their dead with dignity. Initially covering 3.6 hectares (9 acres) of ground, the area of the cemetery has now grown to approximately 50 hectares (124 acres). More than 1.5 million people have been interred here from all walks of life – the rich and famous, paupers, politicians, artists, heroes and patriots. When first established the main part of the cemetery was surrounded by a high wall with watchtowers. The watchmen who patrolled the grounds also had a pack of bloodhounds roaming the cemetery; this action was to deter the scourge of bodysnatchers who were active in the 18th and early 19th century, stealing freshly interred bodies for surgical students. Ireland's tallest round tower was built to house the crypt of the founder Daniel O'Connell and inside a staircase where visitors can climb the 51m (168 ft) to the top. The timeline of our country is literally carved in the stone of this graveyard. Some of those interred here include; Roger Casement, Charles Stuart Parnell, Michael Collins, Eamon De Valera, Countess Markievicz, Brendan Behan and Luke Kelly, to name but a few.

Left: The watch towers were built to deter 'body snatchers'
Right: The O'Connell tower dominates the skyline in Glasnevin
Insert: Wall plaque explaining why the towers were built (FI)

This watch-tower was completed by 1842 to prevent bodies being snatched from Glasnevin (Prospect) Cemetery for anatomical use in medical schools

In his most famous work *Ulysses,* James Joyce (1882 – 1941) created characters, a novel and his own day 'Bloomsday.' The novel follows the movements of Leopold Bloom through one single day, June 16th 1904. Bloomsday (named after Leopold) is now celebrated every year when participants dress in Edwardian attire and visit many of the places mentioned in the book. James Joyce was born in Rathgar and was educated in Clongowes Wood, Belvedere College and University College (then on St. Stephen's Green).

In 1904 the first of his short stories was published and Joyce and his wife, Nora Barnacle, left Ireland for Pula, Croatia, where he got a job teaching English. In 1914 his first novel *A Portrait of the Artist as a Young Man* was published with poet Ezra Pound's assistance. That same year his collection of short stories *Dubliners* was published and he wrote his only play *Exiles.* The start of the first World War saw Joyce, Nora and their 2 children, Giorgio and Lucia, move to Zurich. It was around this time that Joyce concentrated on *Ulysses* and many of the characters closely resemble his family members, friends and enemies. After the war the family moved to Paris and spent the next 20 years there. In 1922 *Ulysses* was published and it was not until 1939 that his final book *Finnegans Wake* was available. The war again dictated his movements and the Joyce family were given asylum in Zurich. Joyce was also an accomplished Tenor winning the Bronze medal in Feis Ceol 1904 and with some businessmen launched Ireland's first cinema, the 600 seater Volta in 1909. James Joyce is buried in Fluntern cemetery, in Zurich.

Left: Portrait of James Joyce (PD)
Right & Insert: Bloomsday celebrated in all its glory (William Murphy)

The Dunsink Observatory was founded in 1783 and is the oldest Scientific Institute in Ireland. It was set up as an astronomical observatory, but with the growth of the city it became limited in its use. It is located on top of a hill in the North-west of the Phoenix Park. The Observatory was adopted as Dublin's meridian (an imaginary circle of the earth used for measuring time). It was often called the Dunsink Meridian or Dunsink Mean Time. In 1880 The Definition of Time Act set Dublin Mean Time as the legal time for Ireland - it was 25 minutes and 21 seconds behind Greenwich Mean Time (GMT). This continued until after the 1916 Easter Rising when the time difference was found inconvenient for telegraphic communication. On 1st October of that year Irish time would henceforth be the same as British time (GMT).

Left: Dunsink at dusk
Right: Dunsink Observatory the meridian for Dublin Mean Time (Ian Carruthers)

Croke Park, Dublin, is the flagship stadium of the Gaelic Athletic Association (GAA). This amateur association boasts one of the largest and most modern sporting arenas in the world. The GAA promotes and organises the development of our national games - hurling and football. They purchased the present site in 1913, it was previously called Jones' Road. The stadium is named after Archbishop Croke of Cashel who was one of the first patrons of the Association. The current seating capacity is 82,300 on 3 tiers with 7 levels. The largest ever crowd to attend an All-Ireland final was 90,556 spectators in 1961 when Offaly played Down. Other notable events that took place here include:

1972: Boxing match between Muhammad Ali and Al 'Blue' Lewis.

1984: The first music concert held at the venue featuring Neil Diamond on stage

2003: The Special Olympic Games with an opening ceremony of 80,000 spectators.

2007: Floodlights were used for the first time at the venue with Dublin taking on Tyrone. Also in this year Ireland and France became the first ever rugby teams to play at the venue and Ireland and Wales became the first ever soccer teams to line out in the stadium.

2011: Queen Elizabeth and the Duke of Edinburgh made an historic visit to Croke Park as part of their state visit to Ireland.

Left: Croke Park as viewed from the canal (Michael Foley)
Right: Croke Park on match day (Philip Milne)

John Butler Yeats (1839-1922), the patriarch of the family was educated in Trinity College and was admitted to the Bar in 1866. His preferred career was painting and he moved several times between England and Ireland to fulfil his commissions. His portrait art work can be viewed in the National Art Gallery (see #44). In 1907 he emigrated to America and is buried in Chestertown, New York.

William Butler Yeats (1865 –1939), Irish poet, playwright and literary figure, was born in Sandymount, Dublin. He was a co-founder of the Abbey Theatre in 1904 and in 1908 founded the Cuala Press with his sisters. In 1923 he was awarded the Nobel Prize for Literature. He became a Senator and was on the committee selecting the first Irish coins. He died in France and his remains were repatriated to Drumcliff, County Sligo in 1948.

The Yeats sisters, Susan Mary (1866-1949) and Elizabeth Corbett (1868-1940) were known as Lily and Lolly. Lily specialised in embroidery and Lolly's talent was printing. They founded Cuala Industries of which Cuala Press was a part – producing over 70 titles. The Yeats sisters are buried in Dundrum, Dublin.

John Butler Yeats 'Jack B.' (1871-1957), was born in London and studied painting and drawing. He moved to Dublin and excelled in his paintings of Irish landscapes and horses. He was a close friend of Samuel Beckett (see # 97) and designed sets for the Abbey Theatre. In 1924 Jack B., Ireland's first Olympic Games medallist, won a silver medal for his painting *The Liffey Swim.* He is buried in Mount Jerome Cemetery in Dublin.

Left: John Butler Yeats (US Library of Congress)
Right: (top left) William Butler Yeats (top right) Lily Yeats (bottom left) Elizabeth Yeats working the Cuala Press (bottom right) Jack Butler Yeats (PD)

W.B. YEATS

124-14

137

St. Stephen's Green was first used as commonage to graze sheep and cattle. Its next purpose was as a leper colony and then it became a place for public hangings. The name originates from a church called St. Stephens which was located in the area in the 13th century, a leper colony was attached to the church. In 1664 the 9 hectares (22 acres) of the park was enclosed with a wall and the residential development of the area began including the stocking of the 'Green' with rare wild fowl. In 1814 the boundary wall was replaced with railings.

During the 1916 Rising the Irish rebels were positioned on the College of Surgeons side, while the British soldiers were near the Shelbourne Hotel. There was one man not happy that the revolution was taking place on his 'Green' and that was the groundskeeper James Kearney. His concern was the welfare of the rare birds and ducks under his care. He walked out each day between the rifles carrying the bird food to feed his charges. Both sides stopped the shootings and a ceasefire duly held until after the birds were fed. When Kearney left the 'Green' the shooting began again.

Left: 'The Green' in full bloom
Right: A busy St Stephen's Green
Insert: Ducks enjoying the sunshine (All Photos Michael Foley)

The Book of Kells is one of the greatest creations of Western Art. It is a masterpiece of calligraphy and beautiful illuminations inspired by the Celtic Art influences. The vellum pages used in the book required the skins of over 180 calves. The colour used by the illuminators came from plants and flowers and included vermilion, orpiment and verdigris. The book is believed to have been made on the Island of Iona, Scotland, which was founded by Saint Colmcille. It contains the four gospels written in Latin. The Vikings raided Iona in the early 9th century and the monks relocated to Kells in County Meath.

The book was completed in this new monastery and remained on display in Kells until 1661 when it was presented to Trinity College Library. Each year over half a million visitors view the manuscript. With the technological age the Book of Kells is now available to view as an 'App.'

Left: Trinity College grounds (FI)
Right: Extracts from the 'Book of Kells' (The Board of Trinity College Dublin)

Molly Malone

In Dublin's Fair City
Where the girls are so pretty
I first set my eyes on sweet Molly Malone
As she wheel'd her wheel barrow
Through streets broad and narrow
Crying cockles and mussels alive, alive o!

Chorus
Alive, alive o!, alive, alive o!
Crying cockles and mussels alive, alive o!

The Dublin Anthem *Molly Malone (Alive, Alive, Oh)* recalls and celebrates the life and times of famed Dublin street vendor of the same name. International Molly Malone Day is June 13th and her famous statue was unveiled in 1988 during Dublin's Millennium celebrations. Molly is located at the end of Grafton Street but is moved temporarily to Suffolk Street while the new Luas tramline is being completed. Legend tells us that Molly was a street vendor who sold fish on the streets of Dublin. She wheeled her wheelbarrow from the Liberties to the fashionable Grafton Street area to ply her trade. While the oral version of the song is uniquely Dublin, a written version was published in Massachusetts, U.S.A. in the late 1800's and acknowledges that the song was reprinted by permission of Messers Kohler and Son of Edinburgh, indicating there must have been an earlier publication of the song in Scotland. Whatever the written origins, the song is a Dublin anthem and can be heard at all sporting venues involving Dublin Gaelic and Soccer teams and is also adopted by the Leinster and Irish Rugby teams. Several movies have used the song in their soundtracks and it has been recorded by artists as diverse as; The Dubliners, U2, Sinead O'Connor and Danny Kaye. True Dubliners will tell you that on certain evenings you may still hear the eerie sound of a handcart travelling Dublin's cobbled streets, wheeled by the unquiet spirit of Molly Malone.

Left: The words of the anthem (David Murphy)
Right: The statue of Molly and her cart (Jennifer Boyer)

MISS ELIZABETH O'FARRELL

Elizabeth O'Farrell (1884-1957) was born at City Quay, Dublin and was an Irish nurse who worked as a mid-wife in Holles Street Hospital. As a member of Cumann na mBan (Irish Women's Council) she took a very active part in the Easter Rising of 1916. She acted as a dispatcher before and during the Rising, delivering bulletins and carrying instructions to all the rebel outposts in and around Dublin. She remained in the General Post Office, along with Julia Grennan and Winifred Carney, until the end of the Rising and cared for the wounded, James Connolly among them. On Saturday 29th April 1916 she was requested to carry out a very historic mission. She was handed a Red Cross insignia and a white flag and was asked to deliver the surrender conditions of the Volunteers to the British Military. She walked out into heavy fire on Moore Street and when the flags were recognised the shooting ceased. She was taken to General William Lowe who demanded the unconditional surrender of the Volunteers. He sent O'Farrell back with the demand. Pearse agreed and accompanied by O'Farrell surrendered in person to General Lowe and his son John Lowe (see #34). O'Farrell, accompanied by a priest and 3 soldiers, was then asked to bring the order of surrender to the insurgent positions throughout the city. She spent several months in prison after the Rising but General Lowe petitioned that leniency be shown for the 'great assistance' she had given in managing the final hours of the Rising.

Left : Portrait of Elizabeth O'Farrell
Right: Extract from the Catholic Bulletin relating to events of Easter Week
Far Right: Padraig Pearse surrenders – look closely at Pearse's feet- you will see the bottom of Elizabeth O'Farrell's dress (All Photos - National Library of Ireland)

attend them. The soldier asked us would Pearse speak to him. Pearse said "Certainly." The soldier then asked Pearse to lift him a little in the bed. Pearse did this, the soldier putting his arms round his neck. This was all. Pearse returned to James Connolly's bedside, and the consultation was continued in private.

Message to General Lowe.—Shortly afterwards, I got orders from Sean MacDermott to provide a white flag—he first hung one out of the house to ensure me from being fired on. I left by the house (Gorman's), 15 Moore Street, about 12.45 *p.m.* on Saturday the 29th, with a verbal message from Commandant Pearse to the Commander

MISS ELIZABETH O'FARRELL.   MISS JULIA GRENAN.

of the British Forces, to the effect that he wished to treat with them. I waved the small white flag which I carried and the military ceased firing and called me up to the barrier which was across the top of Moore Street into Parnell Street. As I passed up Moore Street I saw, at the corner of Sackville Lane, the O'Rahilly's hat and a revolver lying on the ground—I thought he had got into some house. I gave my message to the officer in charge, and he asked me how many girls were down there. I said three. He said, "Take my advice and go down again and bring the other two girls out of it." He was about putting me back again through the barrier when he changed his mind and said, "However, you had better wait, I suppose this will have to be reported." Then he sent another officer with me up Parnell Street, towards the Parnell Statue—he sent into one of the houses there (I think it was 70 or 71 Parnell Street) for some one in command. The Officer in Command then came out.

Elizabeth O'Farrell

145

Dublin was originally called 'Dubh Linn.' The name is derived from the Old Irish Gaelic language and it literally means 'Black Pool'. The 'Dubh Linn' was a dark tidal pool used by the Vikings to moor their trade ships and was connected to the River Liffey by the River Poddle. Today, the Castle Gardens at the rear of Dublin Castle mark the ancient site of the 'Black Pool.'

The name Baile Átha Cliath derived from a Gaelic settlement which was further up the River Liffey near the present day Father Mathew Bridge, which links Merchants Quay to Church Street and the north quays. The translation of Baile Átha Cliath means 'town of the hurdled ford' and described a bank of wooden hurdles built across the River Liffey to allow people to cross at low tide. The settlers constructed lattice hurdles (a framework of interlaced willow branches) and secured it to the muddy bed of the river.

Dublin is in fact the oldest Norse capital in the world – the next contender, Reykjavik, was not established for another 30 years.

Left: Replica of Viking ship that sailed up the River Liffey (Museum of Cultural History, University of Oslo)
Right: 'Dubh Linn,' the site of the 'Black Pool' that gave Dublin one of its names (William Murphy)

A Revolution for Fish and Chips

Ivan Beshov (1883-1987) was born near Odessa on the Black Sea. In 1905 he was working as a mechanic on board the Russian Battleship Potemkin when the crew mutinied against the cruel conditions they were living through. This was the first major show of discontent against the Russian Tsar and became a prelude to the Russian Revolution. The mutiny inspired the Bolshevik Revolution and formed the basis for one of the greatest films ever made *Battleship Potemkin.* When the crew of the Potemkin surrendered to the Romanian authorities, Beshov used forged documents and moved onward to Turkey, London and Ireland. He landed in Dublin in 1913 and the Irish authorities suspected Beshov of being a spy and put him in prison. After his release he worked for an oil company and eventually opened his own cafe on Usher's Quay. He changed his surname to Beshoff, then went on to open cafés in Howth, Clontarf, Malahide, Mespil Road and Dame Street. Beshoff's Fish and Chips have attained a standard in Dublin by which all other fish and chip shops are judged.

Left: Ivan Beshov holds a photograph of himself as a young sailor (Beshoff Bros)
Right: Beshoff's Fish and Chip shop (William Murphy)
Insert: The battleship 'Potemkin' (Beshoff Bros)

Beshoff Bros

FISH + CHIPS

Beshoff's

Fresh Haddock Meal

Fresh Fish 'n Chips Meal

Premium Scampi Meal

North Atlantic Fresh Cod Meal

Natural Smoked Haddock Meal

Scampi

Beshoff Bros

All Day Special

oh My Cod!

Cod Goujons & Fresh Potato Chips

€4.95

ALSO...

Chicken Goujons and Chips

#73　Freedom of the City and Grazing Sheep

The Freedom of Dublin City is awarded to people who have made a contribution to the life of the city or of Ireland in general. Honourees include public servants, politicians, artists and entertainers as well as foreign leaders and the Irish Diaspora. The Lord Mayor presents an illuminated scroll to the recipient and they then sign the roll of freedmen in the Mansion House. The Freedom of Dublin began in 1876 and to date over 80 people have been honoured. The first recipient was Isaac Butt (Irish Nationalist and Home Rule Leader). Millennium recipients, U2 - Bono, The Edge, Adam Clayton and Larry Mullen - took the Freedom Award literally. They invoked one of the rights that came with the ancient honour – the right to graze sheep on St. Stephen's Green. The band arrived with sheep in tow and released them to graze. Onlookers were amused but the groundsmen did not share the civic spirit. Other rights that accompany the Freedom include exemption from taxes charged on goods brought through the city gates and the right to vote in municipal elections. Freedmen had a duty to defend the city and needed to own a bow and sword. Other Recipients include: Charles Stuart Parnell, Bob Geldof, Ronnie Delaney, Mikhail Gorbachev, Bill Clinton, John F. Kennedy, Ulysses S. Grant, Mother Teresa, Nelson Mandela, John Paul II, Stephen Roche, Jack Charlton and George Bernard Shaw.

Left: Bill Clinton and Nelson Mandela both received Freedom of Dublin (PD)
Right: Some of the recipients include, (top l to r) Bob Geldof (Shutterstock), Charles Stuart Parnell (PD) and Mother Teresa (Dreamstime) (bottom l to r) John F. Kennedy, Pope John Paul II and the first recipient of the honour Isaac Butt (All PD)

Grace O' Malley (Gráinne Uaile) was a famous pirate Queen who plundered the passing ships of her County Mayo stronghold. When she felt she was unfairly targeted by the English garrisons in Connaught, she decided to go to the top with her complaint and sailed to London for a meeting with Queen Elizabeth I. On her return to Ireland she called to Howth Castle to pay her respects to Lord Howth. She was refused admission because the family were at dinner and could not be disturbed. Grace was outraged and was returning to her ship when she happened to come upon the Earl's grandson and heir, Christopher St. Lawrence, playing in the gardens. She abducted the boy and took him to her Mayo home, Rockfleet Castle. When the Lord of Howth requested the return of his son, Grace agreed on one condition: that the doors of Howth Castle should forevermore be left open at meal times and no one in search of food and shelter should ever be turned away. The Lord agreed to her conditions and the pledge was honoured for many centuries. To commemorate this event there is a street in Howth called 'Grace O'Malley Road.'

Left & Right: Howth Castle (Des Mooney)

Though Dublin, and indeed Ireland, is unaffected by earthquakes, it seems extraordinary that the father of Seismology was a Dublin-man. Robert Mallet (1810 – 1881) was educated in Trinity College, Dublin and qualified in Geophysics and Civil Engineering. He distinguished himself in the research of earthquakes and was credited with being the first person to use the words epicentre and seismology. In 1849, he detonated kegs of gunpowder under Killiney Beach and then measured the travel times of the shock waves along the sand. Similar tests were carried out on Dalkey Island. These experiments were the world's first in the study of earthquakes. In 1857, Padula, in Italy was devastated by an earthquake that reached 6.9 on the Richter Scale and caused the deaths of 11,000 people. Mallet went to Italy to record the devastation first hand. His report was a major scientific work and was invaluable in the study of the cause of earthquakes. As recognition for his scientific study a crater on the moon has been named after him.

(A.I.F.) Robert Mallet's father, John, owned an iron foundry in Capel Street and they made the iron railings around Trinity College. The foundry also made the original cast iron tower at Fastnet Lighthouse.

Left: Robert Mallet the Father of Seismology (Science Photo Library)
Right: Earthquake damage in Christchurch New Zealand (Steve Taylor Photography)

The Point Depot is located on the North Wall Quay of the River Liffey in the Dublin Docklands. It was constructed in 1878 and functioned as a train depot to serve the busy port nearby. In the late 1980's the disused and neglected depot was bought by local developers, Harry Crosbie and Live Nation. The venue was fitted out with balconies, offices, dressing rooms and backstage facilities. The capacity was 8,500 and 'The Point Depot' was now open for business. International stars, boxers and wrestlers all shared the venue but the greatest exposure came in 1994 when the Eurovision Song Contest was hosted live and the interval act launched *Riverdance* (see #60) on to the world stage. The Point was closed in 2007 for re-development and upgrading and in 2008 reopened as the O2 Arena, the seating capacity was now 14,000, with state of the art facilities for patrons. In 2014 '3 Ireland' bought '02' and the name changed to 3 Arena. Some of the acts to have played in the venue include: Frank Sinatra, Nirvana, Neil Diamond, U2, Bruce Springsteen, Oasis, The Eagles, Fleetwood Mac, Pearl Jam, R.E.M. and David Bowie.

Left: Bruce Springsteen (The Boss), One of the many International Acts to perform at 'The Point.' (Shutterstock)
Right: The new look 3 Arena - concert venue at night time (Joe Cashin)

The Martello Towers are small defensive forts that were constructed by the British Empire during the early 19th century to repel any invasion by French troops during the Napoleonic Wars. The towers were inspired by a round fortress built in 1565 at Mortella Point on the island of Corsica. Somehow, in the translation of the name, they became known as Martello in Ireland. The towers are 12 m (40ft) high, usually with 2 floors and the round structure of solid, thick walls made them resistant to cannon fire. The flat roof was an ideal platform to mount a heavy artillery weapon that could fire without obstruction in any direction. They were manned by an officer and 15-20 men. The British built about 50 Martello towers around the coastline of Ireland. On the East coast, in the Dublin Bay area, 26 towers were built within sight of each other, thus providing the ability to communicate and warn of any attacks.

The Sandycove Tower, near Dun Laoghaire, is possibly the most famous. James Joyce (see #63) shared the tower, for a few days, with his friend Oliver St. John Gogarty. Joyce later immortalised the tower by making it the home of 'Buck Mulligan' in his novel *Ulysses*. The tower is now known as the James Joyce Tower and houses a museum dedicated to Joyce.

Left: The Martello tower in Sutton (FI)
Right: Close-up of Martello Tower at Donabate (Des Mooney)

The ship Helga II was built in the Liffey Dockyard in 1908. She was under the control of the Department of Agriculture and Technical Instruction and worked as a fishery research and protection cruiser. However, in 1915 she was taken over by the Admiralty, fitted out with guns and her duty changed to an 'Armed Auxiliary Patrol Yacht.' She served as an anti-submarine patrol vessel as well as an armed escort for shipping in the Irish Sea. Helga's infamous moment happened during the 1916 Easter Rising. She was anchored in the Liffey and was responsible for firing shells on Liberty Hall and the General Post Office. In 1918 she was credited with sinking a submarine off the Isle of Man and also with saving the lives of 90 people when RMS Leinster was torpedoed off Kish Lighthouse. In 1923 Helga II was purchased by the Irish Free State and renamed Muirchú (Hound of the Sea) and became one of the first ships in the newly established Irish Navy. In 1947 the Government purchased new Corvettes and the Muirchú was sold for scrap to Hammond Lane Foundry. But, the 'Old Hound' sank off the Saltee Islands on its final journey to Dublin - though not before her crew safely evacuated.

Left: The Helga ship (Irish Military Archives)
Right: Damage from the shelling (National Library of Ireland)

The Carmelite Church in Whitefriar Street, Dublin, was built by the Carmelite priest Fr. John Spratt. He was known in Ireland as an excellent preacher and for his work with the poor and destitute in Dublin's Liberties. In 1835 Fr. Spratt went on a visit to Rome and while there was asked to preach in the Jesuit Church. The elite flocked to hear him and his sermons were so well received that he was rewarded with many tokens of esteem. One such gift was from Pope Gregory XVI, who presented Fr. Pratt with the remains of Saint Valentine, a catholic priest who had performed Christian marriages at a time when they were banned. Claudius II, who was Pope at the time, had placed a ban on marriages as he believed married men would not leave their families to enlist in the papal army. Valentine was arrested and imprisoned and then beaten to death on 14th February 269 AD. While in jail he restored the sight of the jailer's daughter and the night before his death he gave her a note which was signed 'From your Valentine'

Fr. Spratt brought the remains of St. Valentine to Dublin and they can be seen on the right hand side of the church near the entrance. The casket sits beneath the marble altar. On Valentine's Day (14th February) many couples about to be married visit the shrine for a Blessing of Rings.

Left: Relics of St Valentine (Bruce Matheson)
Right: Interior of the Whitefriar Street church (William Murphy)

#80   *He Gave Us The Wellington Boot*

Arthur Wellesley (1769-1852), the 1st Duke of Wellington, was born in what is now Dublin's Merrion Hotel. When he was in his twenties his mother once commented "I don't know what I shall do with my awkward son Arthur". However, her awkward son became the British Prime Minister on two occasions and was also appointed Field Marshall and Commander in Chief of the English armies. When questioned about his Irish background he is reported to have answered "Being born in a stable does not make one a horse" although some sources have credited the saying to Daniel O'Connell. His greatest victory on the battlefield was the defeat of Napoleon at the Battle of Waterloo in 1815. He participated in over 60 battles in his military career. In his role as Prime Minister he oversaw and supported the passage of the Catholic Relief Act in 1829. His other claim to fame is that he gave his name to a new type of boot 'The Wellington'. They were based on a leather Hessian boot but Wellington instructed his shoemakers to make them from soft calfskin and cut to fit more closely around the leg, stopping at mid-calf length. They were hard-wearing for riding and smart enough for informal evening wear. The style of the boot caught on and are now often called rubber boots, wellies or top-boots.

The Wellington Monument in the Phoenix Park was erected in his honour and is cast from captured cannon. At 62m (204 ft) it is one of the tallest obelisks in Europe. The Ha'penny Bridge (see #48) was also originally named after him.

Left: Wellington Monument in the Phoenix Park (Thomas Mulchi)
Right: The Battle of Waterloo (PD) Insert: Arthur Wellesley (PD)

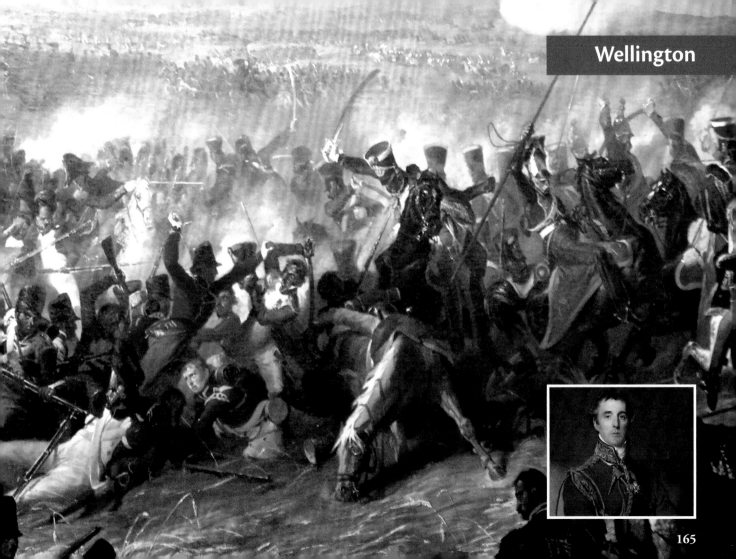

Brian on the Morning of Clontarf.

Clontarf is a coastal suburb on the Northside of Dublin. The name in Irish is 'Cluain-Tarbh' which means the 'Plain of the Bulls'. The Battle of Clontarf in 1014 was an important event in Irish history when Brian Boru, High King of Ireland, freed the Irish from the Norse (Viking) invaders who had colonised Dublin. There was significant opposition to the presence of the Norsemen in Ireland and Brian Boru wanted to unite the Irish kingdoms under one rule and one High King. The King of Leinster (Mael Mordha) revolted and aligned himself with the Vikings and began attacking kingdoms loyal to the High King. Brian set off from Munster and by the time he reached Clontarf he had an army of 7,000 men, facing him was an alliance of 6,600 – Irish and Viking soldiers. The result was one of the bloodiest days in Irish history, with Brian Boru losing up to 4,000 men and the Leinster / Vikings losses were estimated at 6,000, including all their leaders. The High King had won his greatest victory but was killed as he prayed in his tent by a fleeing Viking warrior named Brodir. In Clontarf today Brian Boru Avenue and Brian Boru's Well are reminders of the great battle. In 2014 the Central Bank of Ireland launched a €20 Gold Proof collector coin to mark the 1000th anniversary and a section of the National Museum (see #39) is dedicated to Clontarf 1014. The Brian Boru Harp in Trinity College (see #95) is the symbol of Ireland.

Left: Brian Boru on the morning of the battle (PD)
Right: The battle of Clontarf commences (Hugh Frazer PD)

POBLACHT NA H EIREANN.

THE PROVISIONAL GOVERNMENT
OF THE
IRISH REPUBLIC
TO THE PEOPLE OF IRELAND.

IRISHMEN AND IRISHWOMEN : In the name of God and of the dead generations from which she receives her old tradition of nationhood, Ireland, through us, summons her children to her flag and strikes for her freedom.

Having organised and trained her manhood through her secret revolutionary organisation, the Irish Republican Brotherhood, and through her open military organisations, the Irish Volunteers and the Irish Citizen Army, having patiently perfected her discipline, having resolutely waited for the right moment to reveal itself, she now seizes that moment, and, supported by her exiled children in America and by gallant allies in Europe, but relying in the first on her own strength, she strikes in full confidence of victory.

We declare the right of the people of Ireland to the ownership of Ireland, and to the unfettered control of Irish destinies, to be sovereign and indefeasible. The long usurpation of that right by a foreign people and government has not extinguished the right, nor can it ever be extinguished except by the destruction of the Irish people. In every generation the Irish people have asserted their right to national freedom and sovereignty : six times during the past three hundred years they have asserted it in arms. Standing on that fundamental right and again asserting it in arms in the face of the world, we hereby proclaim the Irish Republic as a Sovereign Independent State, and we pledge our lives and the lives of our comrades-in-arms to the cause of its freedom, of its welfare, and of its exaltation among the nations.

The Irish Republic is entitled to, and hereby claims, the allegiance of every Irishman and Irishwoman. The Republic guarantees religious and civil liberty, equal rights and equal opportunities to all its citizens, and declares its resolve to pursue the happiness and prosperity of the whole nation and of all its parts, cherishing all the children of the nation equally, and oblivious of the differences carefully fostered by an alien government, which have divided a minority from the majority in the past.

Until our arms have brought the opportune moment for the establishment of a permanent National Government, representative of the whole people of Ireland and elected by the suffrages of all her men and women, the Provisional Government, hereby constituted, will administer the civil and military affairs of the Republic in trust for the people.

We place the cause of the Irish Republic under the protection of the Most High God, Whose blessing we invoke upon our arms, and we pray that no one who serves that cause will dishonour it by cowardice, inhumanity, or rapine. In this supreme hour the Irish nation must, by its valour and discipline and by the readiness of its children to sacrifice themselves for the common good, prove itself worthy of the august destiny to which it is called.

Signed on Behalf of the Provisional Government,
THOMAS J. CLARKE.
SEAN Mac DIARMADA,   THOMAS MacDONAGH,
P. H. PEARSE,   EAMONN CEANNT,
JAMES CONNOLLY.   JOSEPH PLUNKETT.

The General Post Office (Ard-Oifig an Phoist), more commonly referred to as the GPO, is the headquarters of the Irish Postal System. It was built in 1818 and was the last Georgian type public building to be erected in Dublin. Standing proud on O'Connell Street it is one of Ireland's most famous buildings, principally due to the events that happened there during the Easter Rising of 1916. Members of the Irish Volunteers and the Citizen Army occupied the building on Easter Monday. Padraig Pearse, leader of the Volunteers, read out the Proclamation of Ireland outside the GPO and declared Ireland a Republic, free from British rule. This action began a week of shelling and combat which led to the near destruction of the GPO and O' Connell Street. The Rising was a military defeat, but public opinion was swayed when the Signatories of the Proclamation and the Volunteer Leaders were executed in Kilmainham Gaol (14 in total) (see #83). It was just a matter of time before Independence was achieved. A fitting tribute to the fallen heroes was erected inside the GPO, it depicts the death of the Irish mythical hero Cúchulainn.

(A.I.F) There were 2 Dublin born signatories of the Proclamation; Padraig Pearse was born in Great Brunswick Street which is now called Pearse Street and Joseph Mary Plunkett was born in Upper Fitzwilliam Street.

Left: The Proclamation of the Irish Republic (PD)
Right: The majestic GPO, symbol of Irelands fight for freedom (FI)
Inserts: (left) Padraig Pearse and (right) Joseph Mary Plunkett (PD)

Kilmainham Gaol was built in 1796 and at that time the front of the prison was used for public hangings. By the 1890's a small cell was built to carry out this death sentence. In the first half of the 19th century, Kilmainham Gaol housed prisoners awaiting transportation to colonies in Australia. Over 4,000 Irish convicts were transported via Kilmainham, their crimes ranging from murder to petty theft. Initially the jail had no segregation policy, with up to 5 men, women or children sharing each cell. They spent most of their time in the cold and dark with only one candle for heat and light. In 1881 it became an all-male prison. Famous leaders jailed there were Robert Emmet and Charles Stewart Parnell. In 1910 the gaol closed but was reopened in 1916 to house hundreds of men and women arrested for their part in the Easter Rising. Between 3rd May and 12th May 1916, 14 men were executed by firing squad in what was called the 'Stonebreakers Yard.'

In 1922 the Free State Army took over the prison and detained anti-treaty supporters in the cells. More executions took place when 77 prisoners were executed as a result of the bitter Civil War.

The Gaol is one of the most important Irish monuments in the struggle for Irish Independence.

Left: Interior of Kilmainham Gaol (Thomas Mulchi)
Right: The Stonebreakers yard where the executions of the 1916 leaders took place (Leo Bisset)
Far Right: The plaque with the names of the 14 executed leaders (Paul Thompson)

ANSEO, TAR ÉIS SEACHTAIN NA CÁSCA, 1916,
BÁSAÍODH NA CINNIRÍ SEO A LEANAS

·

HERE, AFTER EASTER WEEK, 1916,
THE FOLLOWING LEADERS WERE EXECUTED

P.H. PEARSE	3 BEALTAINE, 1916
THOMAS J. CLARKE	3 MAY, 1916
THOMAS MACDONAGH	
JOSEPH PLUNKETT	
EDWARD DALY	4 BEALTAINE, 1916
MICHAEL O'HANRAHAN	4 MAY, 1916
WILLIAM PEARSE	
JOHN MacBRIDE	5 BEALTAINE, 1916
	5 MAY, 1916
CON COLBERT	
ÉAMONN CEANNT	8 BEALTAINE, 1916
MICHAEL MALLIN	8 MAY, 1916
SEÁN HEUSTON	
SEÁN MAC DIARMADA	12 BEALTAINE, 1916
JAMES CONNOLLY	12 MAY, 1916

The Dubliners were an Irish folk band formed in 1962, taking their name from the James Joyce book *Dubliners*. The band attained International success, selling millions of albums, with their lively Irish folk songs and ballads. Band members included; Ronnie Drew, Luke Kelly, John Sheahan, Ciaran Burke and Barney McKenna. In 2012 they celebrated 50 years together and received a 'Lifetime Achievement Award' from the BBC. When Barney McKenna died in 2012 the name 'The Dubliners' was retired from the touring stage.

The Chieftains are a traditional Irish music band formed in Dublin in 1962 and popularised Irish music across the world. They have won 6 Grammy Awards and a 'Lifetime Achievement Award' from the BBC. They were awarded the honorary title of Irelands Musical Ambassadors in 1989. In 1983 they played a concert on the Great Wall of China, the first western musical group to be so honoured. They were the first group ever to perform in the Capitol Building in Washington, D.C. They have recorded with many artists including Van Morrison, Rolling Stones and Madonna.

Thin Lizzy were an Irish rock band formed in Dublin in 1969, taking their name from a character in the Dandy comic. Two young Dublin musicians - bass guitarist and vocalist Phil Lynott and drummer Brian Downey - were original members. They toured Europe and America and their most successful song *Whiskey in the Jar* is a celtic-rock classic still played on radio stations worldwide. Phil Lynott died tragically in 1986 and is buried in Howth, County Dublin.

Left: Statue of Thin Lizzy front man Phil Lynott in Harry Street off Grafton Street (FI)
Right: (top) The Dubliners in art form (Pervaneh Matthews) (bottom) The Chieftains in concert (Paolo Brillo)

It is said a 'True Dubliner' is born between the two canals; the Royal on the northside and the Grand on the southside. These two canals originate almost opposite each other at the mouth of the River Liffey. Construction began on the Grand Canal in 1756, but it took 48 years to connect it to the River Shannon at Shannon Harbour, County Offaly. The canal had three uses in its day; to supply Dublin city basin with water, to enable Guinness to transport its barrels and to supply Guinness with water for the cleaning process. The last working cargo barge made its way along the Grand Canal in 1960. The canal had a number of branches, some of which have been closed while others were restored and are used by leisure crafts. The Grand is 132km (82 miles) long and has 43 locks.

Work began on the construction of the Royal Canal in 1789 and was completed 28 years later in 1817. The total cost of construction was almost £1.5 million. The Royal Canal flows from Spencer Docks to the River Shannon at Cloondara, County Longford. It is 145 kms (90 miles) long and has 46 locks. It was closed in 1955 but was re-opened to navigation in 2010. The Royal never achieved the success of the Grand and the arrival of trains and better roads sounded its death knell. The towpaths, once used by horses pulling the barges, are today being developed as walkways and cycle-ways. Dublin writer Brendan Behan (see #13) is immortalised on the banks of the Royal Canal at Drumcondra Road. Behan's sculpture sits on a bench and his song *The Auld Triangle* is represented by triangles resting on the bench.

Left: A double lock on the Royal Canal (William Murphy)
Right: The serene beauty of the Grand Canal (Thomas Mulchi)

#86   *Downing Street is named after Dublin man*

Downing Street in London has housed the official residences of two of the most senior British Cabinet ministers for more than 300 years. Number 10 Downing Street is synonymous with the Prime Minister, while the Chancellor of the Exchequer's official residence is number 11. This cul-de-sac of two-storey townhouses, with views of St. James's Park, was built between 1682 and 1684 by Dublin man George Downing (1623–1684). Downing left Dublin with his family in 1638 to begin a new life in America. He settled in Salem, Massachusetts, attended Harvard College and was one of nine students in the first graduating class. He became interested in spreading the Gospel and travelled to the West Indies as a preacher. He later arrived in England and became an army chaplain. His career changed many times over the following years as he became a soldier, statesman, politician and businessman. He is recognised as the man who arranged the acquisition of New York from the Dutch and in his honour there is a Downing Street in Manhattan and Brooklyn. As a diplomat he served under Oliver Cromwell and Charles II, amassing great wealth and contacts that enabled him purchase the Downing Street site. His influence in Parliament was substantial and his Navigation Acts strengthened the English naval power and their capability to protect their territories.

His portrait still hangs in the entrance hall of Number 10, Downing Street.

Left: George Downing who gave his name to the street (Harvard Museums)
Right: The iconic Number 10 Downing Street (Shutterstock)

St. Michan's Church was founded around 1095 by the Danish colony of Oxmanstown and is located near the Four Courts. It operated as a Catholic church up until the Reformation. Michan was the spiritual leader of the Danes and gave his name to the church. For 500 years it was the only parish church in Dublin north of the Liffey. The present building dates from 1685-86 and was built to serve a prosperous growing Church of Ireland congregation in the area. The church organ is one of the oldest in the country and it is believed to have been used by G.F. Handel while composing *The Messiah* (see #40). Other items of note include a Penitent's Stool (the only one in Dublin) and a chalice dating from 1516. However it is the vaults underneath the church that are intriguing; coffins can be seen lying haphazardly with body parts sticking out exposing the taut, leathery skin of the deceased. One room holds the coffins of the Sheares brothers who were executed following the Rebellion of 1798; they were hung, drawn and quartered.

The question of why the mummies are preserved is believed to be because of the high concentration of limestone in the walls of the vaults, the low level of the crypt, its nearness to the river and the very dry atmosphere of the environments.

The church graveyard is the final resting place of William Rowan Hamilton (see #38) and Robert Emmet is thought to be interred here.

Left: Exposed bodies in the crypts (Jennifer Boyer)
Right: Looking in at the coffins (Diego Scheid)
Insert: Hauntingly preserved corpses (Jennifer Boyer)

In 1786, John Jameson, a qualified lawyer, moved to Dublin from Scotland to manage the Bow Street Distillery. His wife Margaret was not new to the distilling business as her brothers owned the Haig Whisky brand. The Bow Street Distillery had been established in 1780 and this explains the use of the year in the marketing of Jameson products. In 1810 the company 'John Jameson and Son' was established and took over the ownership of the Bow Street Distillery. Jameson is a blended Irish whiskey produced from a mixture of malted and un-malted or green Irish barley. The barley is dried in a closed kiln before moving into the manufacturing process. When distilled it must be aged for at least 3 years in wooden casks. It has been sold internationally since the early 19th century and is by far the best selling Irish Whiskey in the world, selling over 57 million bottles annually.

Irish whiskey is embedded in our culture to the extent that the Irish word for whiskey is 'Uisce Beatha' meaning 'water of life.' Jameson is now produced by Irish Distillers in Midleton, County Cork. The Old Jameson Distillery in Bow Street, Dublin serves as a museum which offers tours and whiskey tastings.

Left: Exterior of the Old Jameson Distillery (FI)
Right: The old stills in the interior of the museum (FI)

Jameson

FEINTS
STILL
2

SPIRIT
STILL

N°LOW WINES
RECEIVER

THE WORLDWIDE BESTSELLER

A GAME OF THRONES

GEORGE R.R. MARTIN

THE BOOKS THAT INSPIRED THE TV PHENOMENON

GAME OF THRONES

Game of Thrones is a fantasy television drama created by script writers David Benioff and D.B. Weiss. This phenomenal success came about through their meeting in 1995, as postgraduate students at Trinity College, Dublin, while studying Irish Literature. They nurtured their love of writing on the Irish campus with Benioff studying Beckett and Weiss writing his thesis on James Joyce's *Finnegan's Wake*. The pair remained good friends after returning to the US. When they realised they were not going to make a good living in the Literary Arts they turned their attention to fantasy and went back to study Fine Arts in Creative Writing. Television network, HBO, gave them the job of adapting George R.R. Martin's fantasy novel *A Song of Ice and Fire,* to the small screen and thus *Game of Thrones* was born. It is filmed in Northern Ireland, Croatia, Iceland, Malta, Morocco, Spain and Scotland as well as the U.S.A. It has a global audience of 20 million viewers.

Left: George R.R. Martin's bestselling books (Dreamstime)
Right: The cast of the record breaking *Game of Thrones* (Shutterstock)

The River Liffey rises between Kippure and Tonduff in the Wicklow Mountains. It meanders its way through counties Wicklow, Kildare and Dublin. Its total length is 125 km (75 ml). The original name of this famous river was Magh Life (the plain of life), it later became known as Abhann na Life (river of life) and the name Anna Liffey evolved with the Anglicisation of Irish place names. It has 24 tributaries which all add vast amounts of water to the main course. The river has 3 dams which are used for the production of hydroelectric power at Poulaphouca, Golden Falls and Leixlip. About 60% of the Liffey water is extracted for drinking water purposes and to supply industrial uses. Most of this water makes its way back into the river after it is purified in wastewater treatment plants. The Liffey was always used for trade and transport, especially by Guinness Brewery, and is connected to the River Shannon via the Grand Canal and the Royal Canal (see #85). The Anna Liffey is immortalised in novels and song: James Joyce *Ulysses*, Radiohead *How to Disappear Completely*, Charles O'Neill's *The Foggy Dew*, Pete St. John's *Rare Old Times,* Bagatelle's *Summer in Dublin.*

Left: View of the Liffey from Liberty Hall (FI)
Right: The Anna Liffey flows calmly through the capital (FI)

For nearly 800 years the stately home of Malahide Castle was in the hands of the Talbots, except for a brief spell when Oliver Cromwell confiscated their lands. Cromwell gifted the castle to a Myles Corbet. When Charles II came to power, Corbet went on the run but was brought back to Malahide where he was hung, drawn and quartered. His ghost is said to roam the castle in full armour. The ghost of Walter Hussey has a very tragic tale: the morning of his wedding he was attacked and murdered with a spear and his wife-to-be eventually married the murderer. Now his ghost wanders the castle showing his wound. Also sharing in the haunting is a married couple who had a volatile relationship, they dash between rooms usually with the wife chasing her husband. The final spirit is the Puck of Malahide who was the castle jester. He fell in love with one of the castle residents and soon after died under suspicious circumstances but he vowed to haunt the castle forever.

Malahide Castle is the oldest continuously inhabited castle in Ireland. The Talbot family were residents from 1185 until the line died out in 1973; the castle was then sold to the Irish State. A strange happening occurred in the Talbot household on the day of the Battle of the Boyne (1690), 14 members of the family had breakfast in the castle; none were alive by supper-time, all had perished on the battlefield.

(A.I.F.) The castle stands on 100 hectares (250 acres) incorporating a botanical garden of exotic and rare plants from Chile, Australia, Africa and California. The castle is home to the National Portrait Collection.

Left: A haunting view of the castle tower (William Murphy)
Right: The castle entrance (FI)

The Grand Canal Docks have been transformed from a desolate and near abandoned area of the city into a 'Silicon Docks' that is the centre of a technology explosion. World giant computer and media companies have set up their International Headquarters in the Dublin Docklands. Household names like Facebook, Google, LinkedIn, PayPal, Amazon, Twitter and Dropbox are all operating in this Dublin centre. It is now Ireland's central business district and legal quarter with the 2nd highest earning workforce in Europe. These large multi-national companies are attracted to the 'Silicon Docks' by Ireland's highly skilled college graduates and low corporation tax rate. Government agencies, Enterprise Ireland and the Industrial Development Authority (I.D.A), offer excellent advice and funding to start up business ventures locating to the Docks. The Dockland's Strategic Development Zone (SDZ) helps property owners to liaise with the Dublin City Planners.

Left: The new development of the docks area (Thomas Mulchi)
Right: (top) The central business district takes shape (Thomas Mulchi) (bottom) Looking north from the Google building (Michael Foley)

189

In 1908 a bronze statue was erected in the enclosed courtyard of Leinster House, which at the time was owned by the Royal Dublin Society (R.D.S). The statue was a monument to Queen Victoria and was the last royal statue to be erected in Ireland. The eminent artist John Hughes was commissioned to undertake the work and moved his studio to Paris in order to cast the piece. In 1922 Leinster House became the seat of 'The Dáil' (Irish Parliament) and the nationalistic sentiment did not approve of a British Queen in such a prominent location. In 1948 it was removed to the Royal Hospital Kilmainham for storage. In 1980 the queen was moved again, this time to the site of a former children's reformatory at Daingean, County Offaly.

In the mid – 1980's the Queen Victoria Building in Sydney, Australia was undergoing major renovations and an appropriate art piece was sought for the entrance. After much searching by the Australians the statue in Ireland was rediscovered and was given 'on loan until recalled.' The bronze sculpture was 'transported' to Australia by sea and was unveiled in December 1987. It can now be viewed on the corner of Druitt and George Street, Sydney.

Left: Queen Victoria statue now resides in Sydney, Australia (Andy Storr)
Right: The statue when it was in the courtyard of Leinster House
(National Library of Ireland)

QUEEN VICTORIA MEMORIAL. DUBLIN. 9648. W.L.

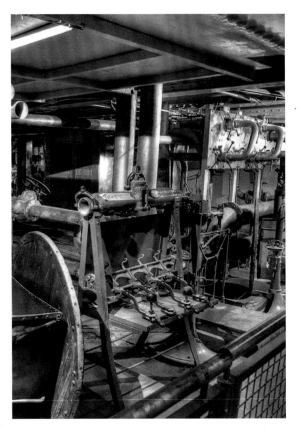

The Guinness Storehouse was built in 1902 and was originally the fermenting plant for the Guinness brewery. It was the first multi-storey steel-framed building to be erected in Ireland and housed the large wooden beer casks that allowed the fermenting process to evolve. It remained as the fermenting plant until 1988 when a new premises was opened. In 1997 the re-design of the old fermenting building began and the newly remodelled and renamed Guinness Storehouse opened as the brewery's visitor centre in the year 2000. The Storehouse covers 7 floors that are designed around a glass atrium mirroring the shape of a pint of Guinness. The history of the beer is explained through interactive exhibitions which include: the ingredients used, the brewing process, transportation and cooperage (barrel making). A newly added feature is a live installation demonstrating the modern brewing process. On the top floor is the Gravity Bar which has 360° unobstructed views of Dublin City and where the famous product may be sampled. In 2015 the Storehouse had almost 1.5 million visitors and in September was named 'Europe's Leading Tourist Attraction', ahead of the Eiffel Tower and the Colosseum.

Left: Old machinery used in the brewery (Marcin Tarkowski)
Right: The storehouse at night (FI)

The Brian Boru Harp is on permanent display in the Library of Trinity College, Dublin. The harp is an excellent example of traditional Irish harps and dates from the late 14th or early 15th century. It was once believed to have been owned by Brian Boru, the High King of Ireland, but he was killed in the Battle of Clontarf (see #81) in 1014. The design of this harp is similar to earlier instruments and this may have led to the belief that it was used in the 11th century. The Brian Boru Harp was the model used by the Irish State as the symbol of Ireland. It is used on all coins, stamps, official government stationary and as the arms of the President of Ireland. Interestingly, Ireland is the only country to use a musical instrument as its symbol. The harp facing left is registered to the Government, while the harp facing right is registered to Guinness (see #17).

(A.I.F.) Trinity College Library holds over 5 million printed volumes and under the Copyright Act, Trinity is legally entitled to a free copy of every book published in Ireland and Britain.

Left: The Brian Boru Harp (The Board of Trinity College)
Right: The Long Room Library (FI)

Brian Boru Harp

Dublin Coddle Recipe

2 pack sausages
8 slices approx. streaky rashers
2 large onions sliced
3 large potatoes
Bunch fresh herbs
Salt & black pepper
Chicken stock
Parsley

Dublin Coddle is a warming meal that dates back to the 18th century. It was a favourite of Jonathan Swift (see #31) and Sean O'Casey. Coddle is mentioned in James Joyce's *Dubliners* and *Finnegans Wake*. The name coddle is thought to originate from the French term *caudle* – meaning 'to boil gently or parboil'. The ingredients for the dish include pork sausages and back bacon rashers mixed with sliced potatoes and onions, in some traditional recipes barley was also added. The ingredients were slowly boiled in a pot or pan containing a small amount of water. The container had to have a well-fitting lid which allowed the steam to cook the contents. The only seasoning was salt, pepper, parsley and in times past a drop of Guinness was also added. Coddle probably originated as an alternative to the traditional Irish stew when mutton was scarce in urban areas and salted bacon and pork was more readily available. Some believe it originated in the days when Catholics were not allowed eat meat on Fridays and on Thursday nights the sausages and rashers that were left over were used to make the dish.

Left: Recipe for Dublin Coddle (David Murphy)
Right: Ready to enjoy (Shutterstock)

Many Dublin citizens have brought honour to the city with their achievement of a Nobel Prize.

1923: William Butler Yeats (see #66)

1925: George Bernard Shaw (see #03)

1969: Samuel Beckett (1906 – 1989), playwright, poet and novelist was born in Foxrock, Dublin. In 1927, he graduated from Trinity College, Dublin with a BA Degree in French, Italian and English. He lived most of his adult life in Paris, France where he became friends with James Joyce. Beckett received two awards from the French Government for his work with the French Résistance during World War II. He is one of the most influential writers of the 20th century. He was awarded the 1969 Nobel Prize in Literature but shunned the presentation ceremony. His greatest masterpiece was *Waiting For Godot.* He is buried in Paris.

1974: Seán MacBride (1904 – 1988) though born in Paris, France, Seán MacBride lived most of his life in Dublin. He is the son of John Mac Bride and Maud Gonne (the inspiration for W.B Yeats love poems (see #66). His father was executed after the 1916 Rising and this inspired his political allegiance to the Irish Republican Army. He studied Law at University College Dublin and was called to the Bar in 1937. He became an Irish Government minister and was a founding member of Amnesty International. He was involved in many other International Organizations including the United Nations and the Council of Europe. He received the Nobel Prize in 1974, Lenin Peace Prize in 1975 and UNESCO Silver Medal for service in 1980.

Left: Nobel laureate Samuel Beckett (PD)
Right: The Samuel Beckett Bridge (Thomas Mulchi)

Clancy Army Barracks is located at Islandbridge, near Kilmainham. It dates back to 1857 and was originally known as Islandbridge Barracks. It had a long connection with the artillery, cavalry and ordnance side of military manoeuvres. The barracks had strong links with military events in the Crimean War, Boer War, World War I and the 1916 Rising. In 1942 it was renamed Clancy Barracks after Peadar Clancy who was killed during the War of Independence in 1920. In 1998 the Irish Government decided that the barracks was surplus to requirement and was put up for sale. Part of the site was developed and the rest lay idle until film companies began to take interest. One of the productions to use the location was the T.V. mini-series *Ripper Street*. The barracks was used to recreate the poverty stricken Whitechapel area of London in the 1890's where Jack the Ripper murdered several women and terrorised residents. Other series to use the barracks were *Titanic: Blood & Steel*, *Shadow Dancer* and *Old Curiosity Shop*.

Left: Members of the cast of *Ripper Street* on location
Right: Dublin transformed to look like Whitechapel in London (David Lynch)

The River Poddle rises in the Cookstown area, north of Tallaght, and flows into the River Liffey near Dublin Castle. The Poddle was given the local name Salach, which is Irish for "dirty or filthy" and over time Salach became Saile. A variation of the name is used in the children's song *The River Saile* (also known as *Weile Weile Waile*). The Dubliners, with Ronnie Drew on vocals, made this song their own and it was sung at his funeral in a tribute by the other band members. The song tells the story of a woman who could not feed her child because of extreme poverty during 'The Great Hunger' (An Gorta Mór 1845-52). The mother killed her child to save it from the terrible suffering of death by starvation. She was arrested, jailed and hung for her crime.

Left: Memorial to the victims of the Great Famine (1845- 1852), located on the quays (Michael Bell)
Right: The Dubliners brought the song to a worldwide audience (Brendan J. Murphy)

In the 12th century, 'Liberty' was a term used to describe a particular freedom or special charter granted to an area of land. The first 'Liberty' in Dublin was granted in 1171 when King Henry II came to Ireland and gave a lease of lands to the Religious Abbeys which were allowed self-rule "owing allegiance to no one but God and the King". The number of 'Liberties' granted increased as more abbeys and churches were founded. 'The Liberties' allied themselves to the city, were self supporting and were responsible for implementing their own judicial system. They gathered taxes, had their own water supply and enjoyed fishing rights on the River Liffey. Most became very wealthy and powerful. 'The Liberties' in Dublin originally included Dolphin's Barn, Harold's Cross, Marrowbone Lane, James's Street, Pimlico, Thomas Street and Meath Street. The Huguenots settled here when they came to Ireland in the early 18th century. They set up small workshops teaching the local people to weave silks and poplin. People of all religions lived together in 'The Liberties' and Irish, English, French, Latin, Dutch and Italian could be heard on a daily basis. By the early 19th century overcrowding and the collapse of law and order resulted in the break-up of the charters and their immersion into the expanding city.

The modern day 'Liberties' is a centre of enterprise and commercial life that is much smaller in area but still includes St. Patricks Cathedral, St. James's Hospital, Guinness Brewery and Christchurch.

Left: Terraced houses in the 'Liberties'
Right: Thomas Street in the heart of the 'Liberties' (All Photos: William Murphy)

Rolling Stone magazine labelled them "The Biggest Band in the World" and it all started in 1976 when Larry Mullen, Adam Clayton, David Evans (The Edge) and Paul Hewson (Bono) began practising in Larry's kitchen in Artane, Dublin. The Mount Temple school friends were first known as Feedback then The Hype and finally U2. In 1979 they joined forces with their now long-time manager Paul McGuinness and in 1980 they found a home in Island Records. Their first album *Boy* was released that year. Their first UK number 1 album was *War* in 1983. They performed and financially supported Bob Geldof in Live Aid in 1985. *The Joshua Tree* album won the band 'Album of the Year' and 'Best Rock Performance' at the 1987 Grammy Awards. Time Magazine featured U2 on its cover, making them the fourth band to achieve that distinction – following The Beatles, The Band and The Who. Released in 2000 the album *All That You Can't Leave Behind* went to No.1 in 32 countries and picked up 7 Grammys on the way. U2 were inducted into the Rock and Roll Hall of Fame in 2005 by Bruce Springsteen who described the band as "being the keepers of some of the most beautiful sonic architecture in the rock-and-roll world." U2 have the distinction of having the most successful concert tour of all time with their 'U2 – 360°' which had 110 shows, attended by 7.1 million fans in 30 countries on 5 continents. They have won a total of 22 Grammy Awards. Another first for the band was iTunes put the album *Songs of Innocence,* free of charge, into the music library of 500 million customers.

Left: The old Windmill Lane Studios – U2 fans sign the wall and leave messages to their idols (William Murphy)
Right: U2 at the Golden Globes (Shutterstock)

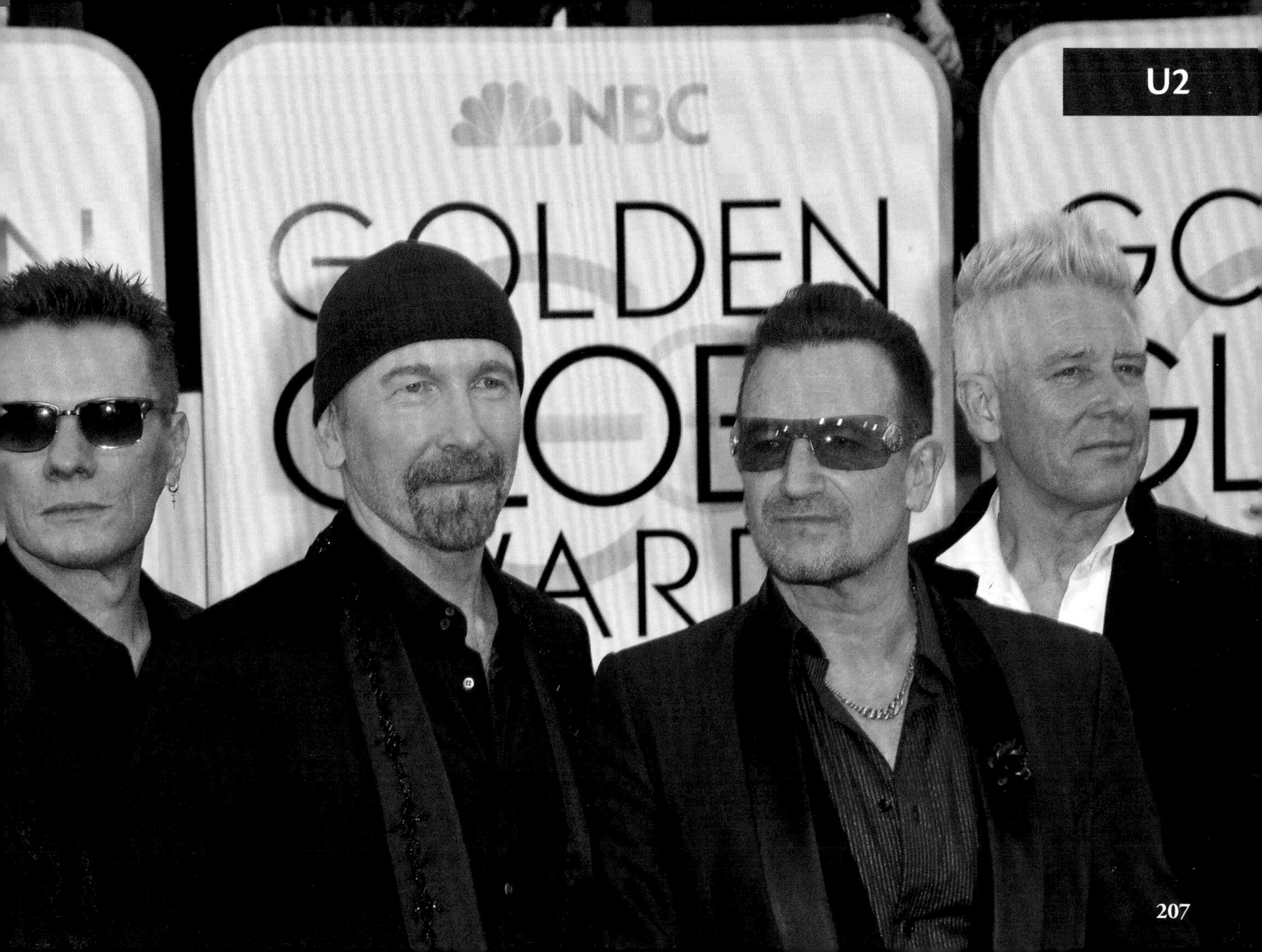

U2

Photograph Acknowledgements

#1 (L & I)) www.wikipedia.org (R) www.shutterstock.com
#2 (L) www.flickr.com - Shay Connolly
   (R) www.flickr.com – Thomas Mulchi
#3 (L & R) www.wikipedia.org
#4 (L & R) www.flickr.com – Danygraig
#5 (L) www.nli.ie (R) www.wikipedia.org
#6 (L & R) www.dreamstime.com
#7 (L & R) www.dublingaa.ie
#8 (L & Far R) www.shutterstock.com
   (R and centre) www.dreamstime.com
#9 (L & R) www.rathbornes1488.ie
#10 (L & R) www.bpl.org
#11 (L) www.flickr.com – Dahon (R) www.failteireland.ie
#12 (L) info@iamirish.ie (R) www.infomatique.org
   (I) www.glasnevintrust.ie
#13 (L) www.flickr.com – Michael Foley Photography
   (R) www.irishcharacterpaintings.com
#14 (L & R) www.sudocrem.com
#15 (L) www.failteireland.ie
   (R) www.flickr.com/photos/34288079@N08
16 (L) Two hundred years of Midwifery 1806-2006 by John F.
   O'Sullivan in Ulster Medical J. 2006 Sep, 75(3): 213-222
   (R) www.flickr.com – mbell1975 (I) www.anpost.ie
#17 (L) www.failteireland.ie (R) info@iamirish.ie
#18 (L & R) www.failteireland.ie
#19 (L) www.flickr.com – Marcus Rahm
   (R) www.flickr.com – Thomas Mulchi
#20 (L & R) www.flickr.com – Síle
#21 (L) www.nli.ie (R) www.melfoody.com
#22 (L) www.wikipedia.org (R top) www.flickr.com – James
   Stringer (R bottom) www.flickr.com – mbell1975
#23 (L & R) www.hughlane.ie
#24 (L) www.infomatique.org (L bottom) www.wikipedia.org
   (R) www.flickr.com – Michael Foley Photography
#25 (L) www.wikipedia.org www.geograph.ie David Hawgood
#26 (L & R) www.flickr.com – Jim Nix/Nomadic Pursuits
#27 (L) www.jeaniejohnston.ie (R) www.failteireland.ie
#28 (L) www.failteireland.ie (R top) info@iamirish.ie (R bottom)
   www.flickr.com paulthompson3747 (I) www.pearsemuseum.ie
#29 (L & R) www.failteireland.ie
#30 (L) www.flickr.com/people/agent-starling/
   (R) www.britishwildlifecentre.co.uk
#31 (L & R) www.wikipedia.org
#32 (L) info@iamirish.ie (R) www.infomatique.org
   (I) www.flickr.com – lonfunguy
#33 (L) www.failteireland.ie (R & I) info@iamirish.ie
#34 (L) www.nli.ie (R) www.wikipedia.org
#35 (L & R) www.infomatique.org

#36 (L) www.wikipedia.org (R & I) www.infomatique.org
#37 (L) info@iamirish.ie (R) www.flickr.com – Stephen Barlett
Travels (FR) www.flickr.com – Josh Thompson
#38 (L & R) www.mpetroff.net (I) www.wikipedia.org
#39 (L & R) www.failteireland.ie
#40 (L) www.wikipedia.org (R top) www.infomatique.org
   (I) www.flickr.com – Stephen Roden
#41 (L) www.failteireland.ie (R) www.flickr.com – Stephen Roden
#42 (L) www.failteireland.ie (R) www.wikipedia.org
#43 (L & R) www.marcintarkowski.com
#44 (L & R) www.nationalgallery.ie
#45 (L & I) www.valeofoods.ie (R) www.floralimages.co.uk
#46 (L & I) www.valeofoods.ie (R) www.nli.ie
#47 (L) www.flickr.com – Cashen
   (R) www.flickr.com – Aidan McRae Thompson
#48 (L & R) www.failteireland.ie (I) www.wikipedia.org
#49 (L) www.nli.ie (R) www.dreamstime.com
#50 (L & R) www.wikipedia.org
#51 (L) www.dreamstime.com (All Rights) www.shutterstock.com
#52 (L & R) www.dublincityofliterature.ie
#53 (L & R) www.largofoods.ie
#54 (L & R) www.cbl.ie
#55 (L & R) www.dublingaa.ie
#56 (L & R) www.nli.ie (Far right) www.shutterstock.ie
#57 (L) www.flickr.com – Michelle O'Connell Photography
   (R) www.failteireland.ie (I) www.nli.ie
#58 (L & R) www.wikipedia.org
#59 (L & R) www.infomatique.org
#60 (L & R) www.riverdance.com
#61 (L & R) www.wikipedia.org
#62 (L & R) www.failteireland.ie
#63 (L) www.wikipedia.org (R) www.infomatique.org
#64 (L & R) www.flickr.com – Landscapeaddict
#65 (L) www.flickr.com – Michael Foley Photography
   (R) www.flickr.com – féileacan
#66 (L) www.wikipedia.org
#67 (L & R) www.flickr.com – Michael Foley Photography
#68 (L) www.failteireland.ie (R) www.bookofkells.ie
#69 (L) info@iamirish.ie (R) www.flickr.com/photos/JenniferBoyer
#70 (L & R) www.nli.ie
#71 (L) www.khm.uio.no (R) www.infomatique.org
#72 (L & I) www.beshoffbros.com (R) www.infomatique.org
#73 (L) www.wikipedia.org
   (Top Left and Right) www.shutterstock.com
   (All Others) www.wikipedia.org
#74 (L & R) www.flickr.com – dmoon1
#75 (L) www.sciencephoto.com
   (R) www.flickr.com – Steve Taylor Photography
#76 (L)www.shutterstock.com
   (R) www.joe-cashen.artistwebsites.com

#77 (L) www.failteireland.ie (R) www.flickr.com – dmoon1
#78 (L) www.flickr.com – Military Archives – code IE/MA/022/033
   (R) www.nli.ie
#79 (L) www.wetaketotheopenroad.wordpress.com
   (R) www.infomatique.org
#80 (L) www.flickr.com – Thomas Mulchi
   (R & I) www.wikipedia.org
#81 (L) www.wikipedia.org
#82 (L & R) www.failteireland.ie (I) www.wikipedia.org
#83 (L) www.flickr.com – Thomas Mulchi
   (R) www.flickr.com – Leo Bisset
   (Far Right) www.flickr.com – paulthompson3747 ·
#84 (L) www.failteireland.ie
   (R top) www.irishcharacterpaintings.com
   (R bottom) www.paolobrillo.com
#85 (L) www.infomatique.org
   (R) www.flickr.com – Thomas Mulchi
#86 (L) www.wikipedia.org (R) www.shutterstock.com
#87 (L & I) www.flickr.com/photos/JenniferBoyer
   (R) www.diegoscheid.com
#88 (L & R) www.failteireland.ie
#89 (L) www.dreamstime.com (R) www.shutterstock.com
#90 (L & R) www.failteireland.ie
#91 (L) www.infomatique.org (R) www.failteireland.ie
#92 (L & Top Right) www.flickr.com – Thomas Mulchi
   (Bottom Right) www.flickr.com – Michael Foley Photography
#93 (L) www.flickr.com – Andy Storr (R) www.nli.ie
#94 (L) www.marcintarkowski.com (R) www.failteireland.ie
#95 (L) www.bookofkells.ie (R) www.failteireland.ie
#96 (L) info@iamirish.ie (R) www.shutterstock.com
#97 (L) www.wikipedia.org (R) www.flickr.com – Thomas Mulchi
#98 (L &) www.flickr.com – Gribers
#99 (L) www.flickr.com – mbell1975 info@iamirish.ie
#100 (L & R) www.infomatique.org
#101 (L) www.infomatique.org (R) www.shutterstock.com